Recipes for Life

National Foundation for Transplants

For additional copies of **Recipes for Life**, call
National Foundation for Transplants toll-free, 800-489-3863.

Copyright © 1997

National Foundation for Transplants
5350 Poplar Ave., Suite 430
Memphis, TN 38119
(901) 684-1697

First Printing	June, 1997	10,000
Second Printing	August, 1998	4,000
Third Printing	February, 1999	10,000
Fourth Printing	March, 2000	10,000
Fifth Printing	June, 2001	15,000
Sixth Printing	June, 2002	5,000
Seventh Printing	July, 2002	10,000
Eighth Printing	May, 2003	15,000
Ninth Printing	May, 2009	4,000
Tenth Printing	December, 2009	4,000
Eleventh Printing	July, 2010	6,000

About The Dividers

All photos shown on the Divider Pages are transplant recipients who are now raising funds, or have raised funds through National Foundation for Transplants.

Bow-Tie Pasta Salad, Grilled Chicken Sesame and Apple Cake with Warm Honey Sauce are reprinted from **Living Well on Dialysis: A Cookbook for Patients and Their Families** with permission from the National Kidney Foundation, Inc.

Some recipes in the Light & Healthy section were reprinted by permission from **Southern Living, Inc.,** Copyright 1991.

ISBN 978-0-9669993-0-3

WIMMER
COOKBOOKS

A CONSOLIDATED GRAPHICS COMPANY

800.548.2537   wimmerco.com

Table of Contents

National Foundation for Transplants and Recipes for Life

Since 1983, NFT has offered fundraising assistance for organ and tissue transplant patients across the country, tailoring our efforts to best suit each individual. We offer assistance to bone marrow and solid organ transplant patients in all 50 states and U.S. territorites from our headquarters in Memphis, TN.

Unfortunately, many transplant candidates and recipients do not have adequate (or any) health coverage or personal savings to pay for their transplant, pre-transplant treatment, follow-up care or medications. Through our effective fundraising and grant programs, NFT offers realistic solutions to meet these financial needs.

Recipes for Life *is dedicated to the thousands of patients and their families who have joined the NFT family. Proceeds from the sale of this cookbook go to a designated state organ or tissue fund, in honor of a specified patient. The funds will be used to help with patients' transplant-related expenses they otherwise could not afford.*

It is fitting that many of the recipes were provided by our patients and their families. They are, indeed, ***Recipes for Life****.*

Thank you for your support. With your help, we are raising hope and changing lives.

National Foundation for Transplants
5350 Poplar Ave., Suite 430
Memphis, TN 38119
800-489-3863
901-684-1697
Fax: 901-684-1128
E-mail: info@transplants.org
www.transplants.org

Acknowledgements

Albright, Debbi
Alderete, Gloria
Alissandratos, A.D. "Andy"
Antes, Sue
Armstrong, Violet
Atteberry, Tracy
Aukerman, Justine
Barnes, Ellie Mae
Bethel, Debra
Billings, Alma
Birks, Carol Tobler
Boiter, Judy
Brazan, Marion
Broyan, Marion
Bruton, Dorothy
Carlisle, Alisa
Carruthers, Eunice
Carter, Dale
Cattarin, Carlo
Cobb, Lee
Collins, Cindy
Conway, Fran
Crump, Bill
Crump, Harriet
Daniels, Marie
Deemer, Carol
Defranco, Judy
Dickerson, Joanne
Dickey, Gloria
Distretti, Jean
Dobrinski, Margie
Doran, Bette
Douglas, Mary Ella
Dulla, Mary Ann

Dyson, Frances
Dyson, Jo Katherine
Ecoles, Tina
Edwards, Hazel Sowder
Elliott, Maria E.
Feingold, Marie
Feland, Jodi
Floyd, Jr. Ben
Floyd, Peggy
Frazier, Elois J.
Fredres, JoAnn
Friend, Marie
Friends in Beta Sigma Phi
Fuller, Viki
Ganoung, Janet
Gentry, Vickie
Gilpatrick, Veta
Goldfinger, Suzette
Gray, Donald A.
Gray, Patricia
Gustafson, Karen
Hall, Truman
Halladay, Helen
Hannah, Christine
Harmon, Jan
Harmon, Terry
Hayes, Carol Ann
Hinkle, Sharon
Hisaw, Lee Ann
Hollis, Tammi
Hopkins, Clara
Horne, Marci
Howsden, Carole

Jackson, Debbie
Jackson, Lois E.
Jermyn, Mildred
Johnson, Joyce
Johnson, Pat
Johnson, Sherri
Jones, Doris
Jorgensen, Kathy
Kellam, Peggy M.
Kellehen, Mary Ann
Kelly, Donna
Ketron, Kyoko
King, Deanette
Kirkpatrick, Sandy
Knoll, Anna
Lansley, Susan
Larkin, Rosemary
Lea, Nancy
Lehr, Bonnie
Lewis, Barbara
Luers, Esther
Lugo, Donna
Marshall, Ginny
Mayeux, Bonnie
Mayeux, Jac
McChriston, Gladys
McDonough, Marilyn
McDonough, Melissa
McDonough, Michael
McNeer, Mary
Mitchell, Jan
Morris, Marilyn
Musolf, Katherine
Nash, Vickie
Newman, Robbin

Parks, Marilyn
Perdue, Beth
Pino, Sheila
Poindexter, Cindy
Polk, John
Popeck, Gay L.
Raines, Sue
Reynolds, Pete
Ridings, Teresa
Ruggeberg, Tammy
Ruggles, David
Scott, Angie
Shaw, Peggy
Shipman, Judy
Slough, Liz
Smith, Bettye
Smith, Danny

Smith, Janet
Smith, Kathy
Smith, Kevin
Smith, Virginia
Solomon, Beth
Spahr, Cindy
Stringfellow, Anna
Stuckmeyer, Valerie
Terral, Byron
Terral, Evelyn
Terral, Shirley
Todd, Loren
Todd, P. Marguerite
Tomkiv, Parania
   "Pearl"
Tomlinson, Debbie
Torrence, Dave

Torrence, Mary
Totty, T.
Traxler, P.D.
Turnbow, Mable
Van Dover, Sylvia
Vannucci, Carolyn
Waite, Joan
Ware, Helen
Wein, Tom
White, Beverly
Williams, Dee Ann
Willis, Jean
Wilson, Dorothy
Winfield, Peggy
Yannessa, Anne
Zimmerman, Gloria
Zimmerman, Zoe

Appetizers, Soups, Salads & Beverages

Brian Barndt

Heart transplant recipient,
2005

Brian proudly displays his gold medals from the 2008 U.S. Transplant Games, where he also gave the invocation. Brian received his heart transplant in 2005 and is thriving today.

Oyster Crackers Surprise

1   package oyster crackers
½   teaspoon dill weed
½   teaspoon garlic salt
¼   teaspoon lemon pepper
    seasoning

1   envelope Ranch-style dressing
    mix
1   cup vegetable oil

Place 3 large paper sacks inside each other to absorb oil. Combine crackers and next 4 ingredients in sacks; shake well to coat. Add oil gradually, shaking well after each addition. Leave in bag several hours, shaking often. Store in airtight containers.

Dried Beef Dip

2   (8-ounce) packages cream
    cheese, softened
1   (8-ounce) container sour
    cream
1   teaspoon Worcestershire
    sauce

½   teaspoon garlic powder
1   teaspoon monosodium
    glutamate
6   green onions, finely chopped
4   ounces dried beef, finely
    chopped

Combine all ingredients in a serving bowl. Chill at least 8 hours. Serve with crackers.

Ham-and-Cheese Snacks

1   can refrigerated crescent rolls
4   thin ham slices

4   teaspoons prepared mustard
4   Swiss cheese slices

Unroll crescent roll dough into 4 rectangles. Place a ham slice on each rectangle; spread ham with mustard. Place cheese slices over mustard, and roll up, starting at shortest side. Cut each roll into 5 slices. Place on a cookie sheet. Bake at 375° for 10 minutes or until golden brown. Serve warm.

Whiskey Wieners

1	pound cocktail wieners	1	tablespoon grated onion
¾	cup chili sauce or ketchup	2	tablespoons lemon juice
¼	cup packed brown sugar	3	ounces bourbon

Bring first 4 ingredients to a boil in a saucepan. Add wieners; reduce heat, and simmer 30 minutes.

Sausage Balls

2	pounds ground sausage	1	large jar process cheese
3	cups biscuit mix		spread

Combine all ingredients in a large bowl. Shape into 1-inch balls. Bake at 350° for 15 minutes.

Pineapple-Cheese Ball

2	(8-ounce) packages cream cheese, softened	¼	cup chopped green bell pepper
1	small can crushed pineapple, drained	1	tablespoon seasoned salt
		2	tablespoons chopped onion
		2	cups chopped pecans, divided

Stir together cream cheese and pineapple. Add bell pepper, salt, and onion. Stir in ½ cup pecans. Shape into 2 large balls; roll each ball in remaining 1½ cups pecans. Chill until ready to serve.

Easy Hot Nachos

Monterey Jack cheese, cubed
Tortilla chips

Jalapeño pepper slices

Place 1 cube cheese on each chip. Top with a pepper slice. Arrange on a plate, and microwave at HIGH 20 seconds or until cheese melts. Serve immediately.

Chili Dip

1   (8-ounce) package cream
    cheese

1   can chili without beans
    Shredded cheese

Place cream cheese in a baking dish. Cover with chili, and top with shredded cheese. Microwave at HIGH 3 minutes or until cheese melts.

Cold Nacho Dip

1   can refried beans
    Avocado dip
½   cup mayonnaise
1   (8-ounce) container sour
    cream
1   package taco seasoning
1   small onion, chopped

2   large tomatoes, chopped
1   (4½-ounce) can chopped
    green chiles
1   (4½-ounce) can ripe olives,
    chopped
1½ cups cubed Monterey Jack
    cheese

Stir together first 5 ingredients. Spoon into a 13- x 9-inch pan. Layer onion and remaining ingredients over bean mixture. Serve with tortilla chips.

Snack Crackers

Grated Parmesan cheese
Buttery rectangular crackers

Bacon slices, cut in half

Sprinkle ½ teaspoon Parmesan over each cracker; wrap each in ½ bacon slice. Place on a broiler rack. Bake at 250° for 1½ hours. Let stand 30 minutes.

Viv's Christmas Dip

1   package dry vegetable mix
1   cup sour cream
1   can water chestnuts, chopped

1   (10-ounce) package frozen
    chopped spinach, cooked and
    drained

Combine all ingredients. Chill several hours before serving.

Corned Beef Rollups

Cream Cheese Pastry
1 cup softened butter
2 cups all-purpose flour
1 (8-ounce) package cream cheese

2 (3-ounce) packages smoked corned beef slices, finely chopped
2 cups (8 ounces) shredded Swiss cheese

Prepare pastry. Cream butter and cream cheese. Mix in flour and form into small balls. Wrap in plastic wrap and chill for several hours. When ready to use, let soften and roll into two rectangles, each ¼-inch thick. Combine corned beef and cheese. Top each pastry rectangle with beef mixture. Fold in ends, and roll up, jelly roll fashion, beginning at a long side. Pinch seams to seal. Place on ungreased baking sheet. Bake at 450° 15 minutes or until golden. Cut into ½-inch slices. Serve warm with sweet hot mustard.

Far Western Salsa

1 (28-ounce) can diced tomatoes, undrained
1 (4.5-ounce) can green chiles, diced
½ small onion, chopped

2 garlic cloves, pressed
½ teaspoon salt
Freshly ground pepper to taste
Dash of hot sauce

Combine all ingredients in a serving bowl. Serve with tortilla chips.

Garlic-Cheese Ball

2 (8-ounce) packages cream cheese, softened
1 tablespoon garlic juice
1 teaspoon monosodium glutamate

1 package thin ham slices, chopped
3 green onions, chopped

Combine first 3 ingredients in a medium bowl. Stir in ham and green onions. Shape mixture into a ball, and chill at least 8 hours. Serve with crackers.

Cheese Ball

1 (8-ounce) package Cheddar cheese
1 (8-ounce) package cream cheese, softened
1 small onion, grated
1 teaspoon garlic powder
2 packages chipped beef, diced

Stir together cheeses until blended; add onion and garlic powder. Shape mixture into a ball, and roll in diced beef. Chill at least 8 hours.

Holiday Pineapple Cheese Ball

2 (8-ounce) packages cream cheese, softened
2 tablespoons chopped green bell pepper
2 tablespoons chopped onion
¼ cup crushed pineapple, drained
2 teaspoons seasoned salt
2 cups chopped pecans

Combine cream cheese, bell pepper, onion, pineapple, salt, and 1 cup pecans. Shape into a ball, and wrap in plastic wrap. Chill; roll in remaining pecans.

Party Cheese Ball

2 (8-ounce) packages cream cheese, softened
1 (8-ounce) package sharp Cheddar cheese, shredded
1 tablespoon chopped pimiento
1 tablespoon chopped green onions
1 tablespoon chopped green bell pepper
1 tablespoon lemon juice
2 teaspoons Worcestershire sauce
1 cup chopped pecans
   Dash of salt
   Dash of cayenne

Beat cream cheese at medium speed with an electric mixer until fluffy; add Cheddar cheese, and beat until blended. Add remaining ingredients, mixing well. Shape into a ball, and wrap in plastic wrap. Chill at least 6 hours. Roll in pecans.

Party Ham Dip

2   (8-ounce) packages reduced-fat cream cheese, softened
1   pound lean ham, chopped
1   teaspoon mixed herb seasoning
2   tablespoons chopped fresh chives
½   cup milk
1   loaf Hawaiian pan bread

Beat cream cheese, ham, and milk at medium speed with an electric mixer until fluffy. Add herb seasoning and chives. Chill 1 hour. Cut off top one-fourth of bread loaf; set aside. Scoop out bread loaf, leaving a 1-inch-thick shell. Fill with dip, and replace top slice. Chill until ready to serve.

Stuffed Mushrooms

½   pound fresh whole mushrooms
1   (4-ounce) package spiced cheese with garlic and herbs
¼   cup canned flaked tuna
1   tablespoon chopped fresh parsley
2   tablespoons dry sherry

Wash mushrooms; remove and discard stems. Combine cheese and next 3 ingredients; spoon into mushroom caps, and place on a baking sheet. Broil (with oven door partially open) 6 to 8 minutes or until lightly browned.

Stuffed Jalapeños

2   (8-ounce) packages reduced-fat cream cheese, softened
1   tablespoon hot sauce
½   teaspoon cayenne pepper
½   teaspoon lemon pepper seasoning
    Seasoned salt to taste
2-3 dozen medium-size fresh jalapeño peppers
    Paprika

Stir together cream cheese and next 4 ingredients, using water to thin, if desired. Chill 1 to 2 hours or until stiff. Cut stems from jalapeños; remove and discard seeds. Spoon cheese mixture into jalapeños, and sprinkle with paprika. Chill until ready to serve.

Shay's Artichoke Spread

2   cups (8 ounces) shredded
    mozzarella cheese
1   cup mayonnaise
1   cup Parmesan cheese

1   teaspoon garlic powder
1   can artichoke hearts, drained
    and chopped

Combine all ingredients, and pour into a quiche pan. Bake at 350° for 30 minutes. Serve with Melba toast.

Creamy Tarragon Dip

1   (8-ounce) package cream
    cheese, softened
½   cup mayonnaise
¼   cup milk
4   teaspoons tarragon vinegar
1   teaspoon sugar
¾   teaspoon dried tarragon

¾   teaspoon salt
⅛   teaspoon pepper
    Carrot sticks
    Snow pea pods
    Romaine lettuce leaves
    Cauliflower
    Zucchini slices

Process first 8 ingredients in a blender or food processor until smooth. Pour into a small bowl; cover and chill. Line a large basket with a deep serving dish or aluminum foil. Arrange vegetables around edges; place dip in center.

Olive Balls

1   cup (4 ounces) shredded
    Cheddar cheese
¼   cup butter or margarine,
    softened

¼   teaspoon Worcestershire
    sauce
1   cup biscuit mix
1   (5-ounce) jar pimiento-stuffed
    olives, drained

Stir together first 4 ingredients until a dough forms. Pat olives dry. Shape 1 teaspoon dough around each olive. Place balls on a baking sheet. Bake at 375° for 10 minutes or until golden.

Guacamole

2 avocados
1 lemon wedge
¼ cup minced onion
¼ cup finely chopped tomato

1 jalapeño pepper, finely chopped
2 garlic cloves, minced

Mash avocado in a small serving bowl. Squeeze juice from lemon wedge into avocado. Stir in onion and remaining ingredients. Cover and chill 1 hour before serving.

Ham-and-Chicken Appetizers

1 cup sugar
1 cup water
2 cups fresh cranberries
¼ cup ketchup

1 tablespoon lemon juice
Chopped cooked chicken
Chopped cooked ham

Bring sugar and water to a boil in a saucepan. Boil 5 minutes. Add cranberries, and boil 5 minutes. Stir in ketchup and lemon juice. Stir in chicken and ham. Serve warm with crackers.

Asparagus-Ham Rollups

4 (6- x-3½-inch) ham slices
4 (8- x 4-inch) Swiss cheese slices
1 (15-ounce) can asparagus (or 1 pound fresh)
2 tablespoons butter or margarine
2 tablespoons all-purpose flour

¼ teaspoon salt
Dash of pepper
1 cup milk
1 tablespoon dry sherry
1 (4-ounce) can sliced mushrooms, drained
Paprika

Layer a cheese slice over each ham slice; trim edges even. Cut each stack lengthwise in half. Divide asparagus into 8 portions. Lay crosswise over cheese. Roll up, jelly roll fashion, starting from a short end. Arrange, seam side down, in a single layer in a baking dish. Cook butter in a saucepan over medium heat until melted. Stir in flour, salt, and pepper. Cook, stirring often, until thickened and bubbly. Gradually stir in milk and sherry. Bring mixture to a boil, stirring constantly; boil until thickened. Add mushrooms, and cook until thoroughly heated. Pour sauce over rollups, and sprinkle with paprika. Bake at 350° for 15 to 20 minutes.

Crabmeat Appetizer Ball

1½ (8-ounce) packages cream
   cheese, softened
2 dashes hot sauce
2 teaspoons Worcestershire
   sauce
¼ teaspoon garlic salt
¼ cup mayonnaise
1 pound lump crabmeat
2 teaspoons lemon juice
½ to ¾ cup chili sauce

Stir together first 5 ingredients. Cover and chill 12 hours. Cover entire surface with crabmeat seasoned with lemon juice. Cover ball with chili sauce.

Cream Tacos

1 pound ground beef
2 (15-ounce) cans chili beans
1 (8-ounce) can tomatoes and
   chiles
1 (16-ounce) process cheese
   spread loaf, cubed
1 (8-ounce) container sour
   cream
   Tortilla chips
   Shredded lettuce
   Chopped tomato
   Shredded Cheddar cheese

Brown beef in a large Dutch oven over medium heat; drain. Stir beans and tomatoes and chiles into beef. Add cheese. Cook mixture over medium-low heat until cheese melts. Stir in sour cream. Top tortilla chips with next 3 ingredients. Spoon beef mixture over top.

Salmon Party Log

1 (16-ounce) can salmon,
   drained
1 (8-ounce) package cream
   cheese, softened
1 tablespoon lemon juice
2 teaspoons grated onion
1 tablespoon prepared
   horseradish
¼ teaspoon salt
¼ teaspoon liquid smoke
½ cup chopped pecans
3 tablespoons chopped fresh
   parsley

Pick through salmon, remove any bone or skin. Combine salmon and next 6 ingredients, shaping into a log. Combine pecans and parsley; roll salmon log in mixture. Serve with crackers.

Cocktail Meatballs

2	pounds ground beef	½	cup milk
⅓	cup chopped onion	2	dashes pepper
2	eggs		Olive oil
1	cup Italian-seasoned breadcrumbs	1	(12-ounce) jar chili sauce
⅓	cup grated Romano cheese	1	(10-ounce) jar grape jelly
¼	cup dried parsley flakes		Juice of 1 lemon

Combine first 8 ingredients. Roll into small balls. Cook in a skillet over medium heat in hot olive oil until browned on all sides. Drain. Combine chili sauce, jelly, and lemon juice. Add to meatballs in skillet; reduce heat, and simmer 1 hour.

Party Wieners

1	(8-ounce) jar grape jelly	3	pounds smoky cocktail wieners
12	ounces chili sauce		

Combine all ingredients in a slow cooker. Cook on LOW 6 hours.

Cheese-Broccoli Soup

3	tablespoons butter or margarine	2	(10-ounce) package frozen chopped broccoli, thawed
1	small onion, chopped	¼	teaspoon dried thyme
1	garlic clove, pressed	¼	teaspoon pepper
3	tablespoons all-purpose flour	1	cup whipping cream
2	cans chicken broth	1	egg yolk
½	cup water	1½	cups (6 ounces) shredded Swiss cheese

Melt butter in a skillet over medium heat; add onion and garlic, and sauté until tender. Sprinkle flour over onion mixture, and cook, stirring constantly, 3 minutes. Stir in broth and water, and bring to a boil. Add broccoli, thyme, and pepper. Whisk together cream and yolk, and add to soup mixture. Stir in cheese, and cook until cheese melts (do not boil).

Shrimp Bisque

1½ pounds unpeeled, medium-size fresh shrimp
3 tablespoons olive or vegetable oil
4 tablespoons butter or margarine
1 large onion, chopped
1 carrot, chopped
1 celery stalk, chopped
2½ cups water
1 cup dry white wine
¼ cup uncooked long-grain rice
1 teaspoon salt
¼ teaspoon ground red pepper
3 chicken bouillon cubes
1 bay leaf
1 (15-ounce) can tomatoes, undrained
2 cups whipping cream

Peel shrimp, and devein, reserving shells. Cook shells in hot oil in a 4-quart Dutch oven over medium-high heat, stirring constantly, until flesh turns pink. Remove shells with a slotted spoon, reserving drippings in Dutch oven. Add shrimp to reserved drippings; cook over medium-high heat, stirring often, until shrimp turn pink (about 3 minutes). Place shrimp in a bowl. Reduce heat to medium; add butter and next 3 ingredients. Sauté until tender. Stir in water and next 6 ingredients; bring to a boil. Reduce heat to low; cover and simmer 15 minutes. Remove from heat. Remove and discard bay leaf. Drain tomatoes, pouring liquid into rice mixture. Remove seeds from tomatoes; add tomatoes and shrimp to rice mixture. Process half of mixture in a blender at low speed until smooth. Repeat procedure with remaining mixture. Return mixture to Dutch oven; stir in whipping cream. Cook over medium heat just until boiling.

Quick Minestrone

2 cans condensed beef broth
3 cans water
1 (16-ounce) can tomato sauce
1 can kidney beans, drained
1 package frozen mixed vegetables
1 potato, diced
1 zucchini, diced
½ teaspoon dried thyme
¼ teaspoon marjoram
1 bay leaf
2 teaspoons instant minced onion
½ teaspoon celery seed
½ teaspoon dried basil
¼ teaspoon garlic powder
4 ounces uncooked shell pasta
Parmesan cheese

Cook first 14 ingredients in a Dutch oven over medium-low heat, stirring occasionally, 15 to 20 minutes. Stir in pasta; cook until pasta is tender. Remove and discard bay leaf. Top each serving with Parmesan cheese.

Lentil Soup

1	cup dried lentils	½	cup diced carrot
2½	cups water	1	onion, diced
2	beef bouillon cubes	½	teaspoon dried thyme
1	(12-ounce) can beer	1	teaspoon salt
½	cup diced celery		

Bring first 3 ingredients to a boil in a Dutch oven. Remove from heat, cover, and let stand 1 hour. Add remaining ingredients; cook over medium-low heat 1 hour and 15 minutes.

Chicken Soup

1	(2-pound) chicken, stewed, with broth	2	cups sliced celery
8	chicken bouillon cubes	2	cups sliced carrot
4	ounces medium egg noodles	1	tablespoon sugar
		¼	teaspoon pepper

Remove chicken from bones; set aside. In a large Dutch oven, add enough water to broth to measure 3 quarts. Bring mixture to a boil; add bouillon cubes, stirring until cubes dissolve. Add noodles and next 4 ingredients. Cook until vegetables are tender.

Cabbage-Beef Soup

1	pound ground beef	1	(8-ounce) can tomato sauce
1	medium onion, chopped		Salt and pepper to taste
1	medium-sized green bell pepper, chopped	1	envelope chili seasoning mix
1	large can tomatoes	1	medium cabbage, shredded
		2½	cups water

Brown beef in a large skillet; drain. Add onion and bell pepper; sauté until crisp-tender. Add tomatoes and remaining ingredients. Bring to a boil; boil until cabbage is tender.

Cream of Broccoli Soup

1	(10-ounce) package frozen chopped broccoli, thawed	¼	teaspoon dried thyme Dash of ground red pepper
1	(10¾-ounce) can cream of chicken soup	½	cup (2 ounces) shredded Cheddar cheese
1	can water		

Cook first 5 ingredients, covered, in a 2-quart saucepan over medium-low heat 10 minutes. Stir in cheese; cook until cheese melts.

7-Layer Salad

1	head lettuce, broken into chunks		Mayonnaise (enough to cover)
2	medium onions, thinly sliced	3	tablespoons sugar
6	celery stalks, chopped	½	pound Cheddar cheese, shredded
2	small cans young English peas, cooked and cooled	6	bacon slices, cooked and chopped

Layer ingredients in a 13- x 9-inch dish. Cover with plastic wrap, and chill at least 8 hours.

Shoepeg Corn Salad

4	celery stalks, chopped	2	cans white shoepeg corn, drained
½	green bell pepper, chopped	1	cup non-oil dressing
1	bunch green onions, sliced		Freshly ground pepper
1	(2-ounce) jar diced pimiento		Garlic powder to taste

Combine all ingredients; cover and chill at least 8 hours.

Beth's Aunt Dottie's Bean Salad

¾	cup apple cider vinegar	1	tablespoon Worcestershire sauce
2	tablespoons grated onion		Juice of 1 lemon
1	teaspoon pepper	1	can kidney beans, drained
1	garlic clove, pressed	2	cans French-cut green beans, drained
¾	cup vegetable oil		
¾	cup sugar		
1	teaspoon salt		

Combine first 9 ingredients; stir in beans. Chill 12 to 24 hours.

Pasta Salad

16 ounces rotini, cooked
2 green bell peppers, chopped
1 celery stalk, chopped
½ pound hard salami, diced
½ pound pepperoni, diced
½ pound provolone cheese, diced

½ (2¼-ounce) jar sliced ripe olives
Onion salt to taste
½ teaspoon dried oregano
1 large bottle Italian salad dressing

Combine all ingredients. Chill.

Marinated Mushrooms

Whole fresh mushrooms   Italian salad dressing

Wash mushrooms and place into a bowl. Add dressing, and toss gently. Chill at least 8 hours.

Colorful Coleslaw

¼ green cabbage, shredded
¼ red cabbage, shredded
3 carrots, grated
¼ cup pineapple chunks

¼ cup sugar
3 tablespoons pineapple juice
¼ cup chopped walnuts
Mayonnaise

Combine first 7 ingredients; fold in mayonnaise until all ingredients are moistened.

Rice-and-Bean Salad

1 cup long-grain rice, cooked
3 celery stalks, thinly sliced
4 tablespoons vegetable oil
1 (17-ounce) can red kidney beans, drained

2 tablespoons red wine vinegar
¾ teaspoon salt
½ teaspoon sugar

Place rice in a large bowl, and set aside. Sauté celery in 2 tablespoons hot oil in a skillet until tender. Spoon celery into bowl with rice. Stir remaining 2 tablespoons oil, beans, and remaining ingredients into rice mixture. Serve chilled or at room temperature.

Hot Potato Salad

6	medium potatoes	3	tablespoons sugar
1	small onion, minced	½	cup water
6	bacon slices	1½	teaspoons salt
2	tablespoons all-purpose flour	⅛	teaspoon pepper
⅓	cup cider vinegar		

Bring potatoes to a boil in water to cover over medium-high heat; boil until tender. Cool, peel, and slice potatoes; place in a 2-quart baking dish. Sprinkle onion over top. Dice bacon; cook in a large skillet over medium heat until crisp. Add flour to skillet, and cook until bubbly. Add vinegar and remaining ingredients. Bring mixture to a boil; boil 2 minutes. Pour over potato slices, and stir. Bake at 350° for 20 minutes.

Taco Salad

3	pounds ground beef or turkey	1	large head lettuce, shredded
2	medium onions, chopped	1	pound cheese, shredded
2	envelopes taco seasoning mix	1	onion, diced
¾	cup water	2	packages tortilla chips,
	Salt and pepper to taste		crushed
3	cans chili beans		Picante sauce

Brown beef in a large skillet over medium-high heat; drain. Add chopped onion, seasoning mix, and water. Reduce heat, and simmer 30 minutes. Salt and pepper to taste. Stir in chili beans; cook until thoroughly heated. Place in a serving dish, and add lettuce and next 3 ingredients; stir gently. Top with picante sauce.

Polly Smiths Hot Chicken Salad

8	cups chopped, cooked chicken	8	hard-cooked eggs, chopped
2	(10¾-ounce) cans cream of	3	cups cooked long-grain rice
	chicken soup		Salt and pepper to taste
1	(10¾-ounce) can cream of	2	teaspoons dried oregano
	mushroom soup		Garlic salt to taste
4	cups chopped celery		Shredded Cheddar cheese
¾	cup chopped onion	1	large bag potato chips,
2¼	cups mayonnaise		crushed
4	tablespoons lemon juice		

Combine first 12 ingredients; chill at least 1 hour. Spoon into 2 (13- x 9-inch) baking dishes. Bake at 400° for 25 minutes. Top evenly with cheese and chips; bake 15 more minutes.

Hot Chicken Salad

3 cups diced celery
3 cups chopped cooked chicken
1 cup cubed cheese
1 small onion, diced

1 small green bell pepper, diced
1½ cups mayonnaise
1 cup chopped almonds
1 (2-ounce) jar diced pimiento

Combine all ingredients. Pour into a 13- x 9-inch baking dish. Bake at 350° for 30 minutes.

Sauerkraut Salad

1 cup sugar
½ cup white vinegar
1 cup vegetable oil
1 quart sauerkraut, drained
1 onion, chopped

2 carrots, chopped
1 green bell pepper, chopped
1 (4-ounce) jar diced pimiento, drained
1 cup diced celery

Cook first 3 ingredients in a small saucepan over medium heat until sugar dissolves. Place sauerkraut and next 5 ingredients in a bowl; pour sugar mixture over top, and stir until blended.

Broccoli Salad

2 bunches broccoli, cut up
½ cup raisins
½ cup sunflower kernels
4 bacon slices, cooked and crumbled

1 cup mayonnaise
3 tablespoons sugar
2 tablespoons lemon juice

Combine first 4 ingredients in a bowl. Stir together mayonnaise, sugar, and lemon juice. Fold into broccoli mixture. Chill.

Artichoke Salad

1 box chicken-flavored rice mix
1 (14¾-ounce) jar marinated artichokes, drained and chopped
1 can sliced water chestnuts

3 green onions, chopped
1 green bell pepper, chopped
½ cup chopped ripe olives
Dash of pepper
Mayonnaise

Prepare rice mix according to package directions; cool. Stir in next 6 ingredients and enough mayonnaise to moisten. Chill.

Spaghetti Salad

Cooked spaghetti, cooled and drained
Chopped tomato
Chopped onion
Chopped green bell pepper
Italian salad dressing
Dried salad seasonings
Sliced ripe olives

Place spaghetti in a serving bowl. Add vegetables, and toss with dressing and seasonings. Top with olives.

Black Cherry Gelatin Mold

1 can dark sweet pitted cherries
1 (8-ounce) can pineapple tidbits
1 can mandarin oranges
1 large box black cherry gelatin
1 large box strawberry gelatin
1 (8-ounce) container frozen whipped topping, thawed

Prepare gelatin. Mix as listed, and pour into a mold. Chill at least 8 hours. Unmold onto a large lettuce-lined plate. Spoon whipped topping in center.

Molded Maytime Salad

1 small box lemon gelatin
½ teaspoon salt
1½ cups hot water
2 tablespoons white vinegar
2 teaspoons grated onion
Dash of pepper
⅔ cup grated carrot
¼ cup finely chopped green bell pepper
Cottage cheese
Paprika
Grated carrot

Dissolve gelatin and salt in hot water. Add vinegar, onion, and pepper; stir until slightly thickened. Fold in carrot and bell pepper. Turn into individual molds or a glass serving dish. Chill until set. Dollop each serving with cottage cheese; sprinkle cheese with paprika and grated carrot.

Fruity Gelatin Salad

2 cups cottage cheese
1 small box gelatin (any flavor)
1 (16-ounce) can mixed fruit, drained
1 cup frozen whipped topping, thawed

Combine all ingredients in a serving bowl, and chill until set.

Pineapple Salad

1	large can sliced pineapple	4	tablespoons pineapple juice
1	pound marshmallows	2	teaspoons white vinegar
1	cup pecans	2	teaspoons sugar
1	egg	1	pint whipping cream

Cut first 3 ingredients into small pieces, and place into a large bowl. Place a cast-iron skillet over medium heat. Break egg into skillet; quickly add pineapple juice, stirring constantly. Add vinegar and sugar, stirring until mixture thickens. Pour egg mixture over pineapple mixture, stirring until blended. Beat whipping cream at high speed with an electric mixer until stiff peaks form. Fold into pineapple mixture. Chill.

Gelatin Delight

1	small box strawberry gelatin	1	(8-ounce) container frozen whipped topping, thawed
2	cups boiling water		
2	pints frozen strawberries, thawed and mashed	1	(8-ounce) container cream cheese, softened
1	small can crushed pineapple, undrained	1	cup powdered sugar
		½	teaspoon vanilla extract
4	bananas, mashed		Pecan halves

Stir together gelatin and boiling water in a large serving bowl until gelatin dissolves. Add strawberries, pineapple, and mashed banana. Chill, uncovered, until set. Combine whipped topping and next 3 ingredients; spread over gelatin. Top with pecan halves just before serving.

Can be made with sugar-free gelatin and artificial sweetener instead of powdered sugar.

Orange Delight Salad

1	(16-ounce) box orange gelatin	1	small can mandarin oranges, drained
2	cups boiling water		
1	(16-ounce) can orange juice	1	package lemon pudding mix
1	(20-ounce) can crushed pineapple, drained	1	cup milk
		1	(8-ounce) container frozen whipped topping, thawed

Dissolve gelatin in boiling water. Add orange juice; chill until consistency of beaten egg white. Stir in mandarin oranges and pineapple. Chill until set. Combine pudding mix and milk; fold in whipped topping. Spread mixture over gelatin, and chill.

Apple Crunch Salad

1 large box strawberry gelatin	1 cup peeled, chopped apple
1¾ cups boiling water	½ cup chopped pecans
1½ cups apple juice	½ cup chopped celery
¼ teaspoon ground cinnamon	

Dissolve gelatin in boiling water. Stir in apple juice and cinnamon. Chill until consistency of beaten egg white. Stir in remaining ingredients; pour into a lightly oiled 8-inch square pan. Chill 8 hours or until set.

Peach Fluff Salad

½ cup mayonnaise	¼ cup maraschino cherries, chopped
13 ounces cream cheese, softened	8 peach halves
¼ cup pecans, chopped	Lettuce leaves

Stir together mayonnaise and cream cheese in a bowl until blended. Stir in pecans and cherries. Spoon mixture into peach halves, and serve on lettuce-lined salad plates.

Easy Fruit Salad

1 (8-ounce) container sour cream	1 cup fruit cocktail, drained
2 cups miniature marshmallows	½ cup pecans, chopped

Combine all ingredients, and chill.

Sunset Salad

1 small box lemon or orange-pineapple gelatin	1 (8¾-ounce) can crushed pineapple or pineapple tidbits, undrained
½ teaspoon salt	1 tablespoon lemon juice
1½ cups boiling water	1 cup coarsely grated carrot
	⅓ cup chopped pecans

Dissolve gelatin and salt in boiling water. Add pineapple and lemon juice, and chill until consistency of beaten egg white. Fold in carrot and pecans. Pour into individual molds or a 1-quart glass dish.

Cranberry Salad

2	oranges	⅛	teaspoon salt
2½	cups fresh cranberries	1½	cups finely chopped celery
3	small boxes orange gelatin	1	cup crushed pineapple,
3	cups boiling water		undrained
2	tablespoons lemon juice	½	cup chopped walnuts
1	cup sugar		

Peel oranges. Process orange peel and cranberries in a food processor until finely chopped. Remove white membrane from orange, and separate into sections. Break each section into 3 or 4 pieces. Dissolve gelatin in boiling water; add lemon juice, sugar, and salt. Stir until sugar and salt dissolve. Add celery and remaining ingredients; pour into individual molds or a glass dish, and chill until set.

This salad should be made at least 2 days before serving.

Cranberry Holiday Salad

1	large box raspberry gelatin	⅔	cup fruit juice
1	cup hot water	½	cup chopped walnuts
1	(16-ounce) can whole-berry	2	(3-ounce) packages cream
	cranberry sauce		cheese, softened
1	(13-ounce) can crushed	1	cup sour cream
	pineapple, undrained		Lettuce leaves

Dissolve gelatin in hot water. Pour into a 13- x 9-inch pan. Stir in cranberry sauce and next 3 ingredients. Chill until set. Beat cream cheese and sour cream at medium speed with an electric mixer until smooth. Spread over salad, and chill 30 minutes.

Frosty Cranberry Salad

1	(16-ounce) can whole-berry	1	cup sour cream
	cranberry sauce	¼	cup powdered sugar
1	(8.5-ounce) can crushed	2	pineapple slices, halves
	pineapple, drained		

Combine cranberry sauce and pineapple. Stir together sour cream and sugar; add to fruit mixture. Line a 9- x 5-inch pan with aluminum foil; pour in fruit mixture. Freeze until firm. To serve, turn frozen salad out onto a serving dish, and let stand until a knife can slice through. Cut into wedges. Garnish with pineapple slices, if desired.

Pistachio Salad

1 package pistachio pudding mix
1 (8-ounce) container frozen whipped topping, thawed
1 can crushed pineapple, drained
2 cups miniature marshmallows
1 cup chopped pistachios

Sprinkle pudding mix over whipped topping in a large bowl; stir mixture until blended. Add remaining ingredients, and chill.

Frozen Fruit Salad

1 (20-ounce) can crushed pineapple, undrained
½ cup sugar
1 quart fresh strawberries, sliced
1 (6-ounce) can frozen orange juice concentrate, thawed
2 tablespoons lemon juice
1 (17-ounce) can apricots, drained and diced
3 medium bananas, diced

Drain pineapple, reserving 1 cup juice. Bring reserved juice and sugar to a boil in a saucepan. Add strawberries and remaining ingredients, stirring until blended. Spoon into 36 paper-lined muffin cups, and freeze until firm. Remove from pans. To make ahead, store in zip-top plastic bags in freezer; let stand 10 to 20 minutes before serving.

Fruity Salad

1 large box gelatin (any flavor)
1 (12-ounce) container cottage cheese
1 (8-ounce) container frozen whipped topping, thawed
1 small can pineapple chunks, drained

Combine cottage cheese and whipped topping in a large serving bowl. Add pineapple and gelatin. Chill until set.

Fruit-and-Lettuce Salad

1 cup reduced-fat mayonnaise
3 tablespoons sugar
1 head lettuce, broken into chunks
3 bananas, sliced
2 cups miniature marshmallows

Combine sugar and mayonnaise. Stir together lettuce, banana, and marshmallows in a large serving bowl; stir in mayonnaise mixture.

Avocado Salad

1 small box lemon or lime gelatin	½ cup sour cream
1½ teaspoons grated onion	½ cup mayonnaise
¾ teaspoon salt	1 large avocado, mashed

Prepare gelatin according to package directions; chill until consistency of unbeaten egg white. Combine onion and next 4 ingredients; add to gelatin. Chill until set. Serve with orange or grapefruit sections.

Cinnamon Applesauce Salad

9 ounces lemon gelatin	¾ cup chopped walnuts
¾ cup red cinnamon candies	1 (8-ounce) package cream cheese, softened
4½ cups boiling water	
3 cups applesauce	⅓ cup milk
1½ tablespoons lemon juice	3 tablespoons mayonnaise
Dash of salt	

Dissolve gelatin and candies in boiling water in a large bowl. Stir in applesauce, lemon juice, and salt. Chill until consistency of beaten egg white. Add walnuts, and pour into a 13- x 9-inch pan. Stir together cream cheese, milk, and mayonnaise; spread over gelatin, swirling to marble.

Pretzel Salad

2⅔ cups crushed pretzels	1 (12-ounce) container frozen whipped topping, thawed
3 tablespoons sugar	
¾ cup butter or margarine, melted	1 cup sugar
	1 large box strawberry gelatin
1 (8-ounce) package cream cheese, softened	3 cups boiling water
	1 large box frozen strawberries
	Crushed pretzels

Combine 2⅔ cups crushed pretzels, 3 tablespoons sugar, and butter; press into a 13- x 9-inch pan. Bake at 350° for 10 minutes. Cool. Combine cream cheese, whipped topping, and 1 cup sugar; spread mixture over crumb crust. Dissolve gelatin in boiling water; stir in strawberries, and let thicken slightly. Pour gelatin mixture over cream cheese layer; sprinkle with crushed pretzels.

Red, White, and Blue Salad

2   small boxes red raspberry
    gelatin
3   cups boiling water, divided
1   envelope unflavored gelatin
½   cup cold water
1   cup milk
1   cup sugar

1   teaspoon vanilla extract
1   (8-ounce) package cream
    cheese, softened
1   cup chopped walnuts
1   (16-ounce) can blueberries in
    syrup, undrained

Dissolve 1 box raspberry gelatin in 2 cups boiling water. Pour into a 13- x 9-inch pan. Chill until set. Dissolve unflavored gelatin in cold water. Cook milk and sugar in a saucepan until scalded; stir into unflavored gelatin. Add vanilla and cream cheese, stirring until well blended. Cool slightly, and stir in walnuts. Pour cream cheese mixture over raspberry gelatin. Chill until set. Dissolve remaining box raspberry gelatin in remaining 1 cup boiling water. Add blueberries, and pour over cream cheese layer. Chill until set.

Ribbon Salad

4   small boxes gelatin (any
    flavor)
4   cups boiling water, divided
2   cups cold water
2   cups whole milk

1   cup sugar
2   envelopes unflavored gelatin
½   cup cold water
2   cups sour cream
2   teaspoons vanilla extract

Dissolve 1 box gelatin in 1 cup boiling water; stir in ½ cup cold water. Pour into a greased 13- x 9-inch glass baking dish. Chill 30 to 45 minutes. Bring milk to a boil in a saucepan, and remove from heat; add sugar, stirring until sugar dissolves. Dissolve unflavored gelatin in ½ cup cold water; stir into milk mixture. Add sour cream and vanilla. Beat mixture at low speed with an electric mixer just until blended. Cool. Carefully spoon ⅓ sour cream mixture onto chilled gelatin layer. Chill 35 to 40 minutes. Repeat procedure for first two layers twice; top with a gelatin layer.

Strawberry Salad

1   small box strawberry gelatin
1   cup boiling water
1   banana

1   (10-ounce) package frozen
    sliced strawberries, thawed
1½ cups crushed pineapple

Dissolve gelatin in boiling water. Process banana in a blender until smooth. Add banana, strawberries, and pineapple to gelatin. Chill until set.

Lime-Pimiento Cheese Salad

1	large box lime gelatin	2	cups finely chopped celery
2	cups boiling water	1	cup chopped pecans
1	jar pimiento cheese spread	½	pint whipping cream
1	small can crushed pineapple, undrained		

Dissolve gelatin in boiling water. Stir in cheese spread, stirring until spread melts. Add pineapple, celery, and pecans. Chill until consistency of beaten egg white. Beat whipping cream at high speed with an electric mixer until stiff peaks form. Fold into gelatin mixture; pour into a mold, and chill until set.

Red Cabbage Salad

1	red cabbage, chopped	½	cup vegetable oil
6	green onions	¼	cup rice vinegar
¾	cup slivered almond, toasted	2	tablespoons sugar
2	tablespoons sesame seeds	½	teaspoon monosodium
1	package chicken-flavored ramen noodle soup mix		glutamate

Combine first 4 ingredients; break up noodles from soup mix, and stir into cabbage mixture. Combine oil, vinegar, sugar, monosodium glutamate, and soup seasoning packet; pour over salad. Chill at least 1 hour.

Vegetable Salad

1	cup sugar	1	can early English peas, drained
½	cup vegetable oil		
¾	cup white vinegar	1	cup chopped celery
1	can French-cut green beans, drained	1	cup chopped onion
1	can whole kernel corn, drained	1	cup chopped green bell pepper
			Diced pimiento (optional)
			Chopped carrot (optional)

Cook first 3 ingredients in a saucepan over medium heat just until sugar dissolves. Cool. Combine sugar mixture, green beans, and remaining ingredients. Chill at least 8 hours.

Sweet Potato Salad

4½ cups mashed sweet potato
4 green onions, sliced
1½ cups diced celery
4 hard-cooked eggs, chopped

½ cup mayonnaise
½ cup Durkee sauce
1 teaspoon salt

Combine all ingredients, and chill 4 to 6 hours.

Chicken-Fruit Salad

5 cups chopped cooked chicken
2 tablespoons vegetable oil
2 tablespoons orange juice
1 teaspoon salt
3 cups cooked rice
1½ cups reduced-fat mayonnaise

1 cup toasted almonds
1½ cups green grape halves
1½ cups diced celery
1 (13-ounce) can pineapple tidbits, drained
1 can mandarin oranges

Combine first 3 ingredients; chill several hours or overnight. Stir in salt and remaining ingredients.

Poppy Seed Dressing

½ cup sugar
1½ teaspoons dry mustard
1 teaspoon salt
½ small onion, chopped

½ cup white vinegar
½ cup vegetable oil
½ teaspoon poppy seeds

Process all ingredients in a blender; chill 8 hours.

Creamy Herb Vinaigrette

2 garlic cloves, pressed
1 cup olive oil
1 teaspoon Dijon mustard
1 tablespoon water
1 egg white

⅓ cup red wine vinegar
¼ teaspoon dried oregano
¼ teaspoon dried basil
Pinch of marjoram
Salt and freshly ground pepper to taste

Process all ingredients in a blender or food processor 15 seconds or until smooth, adding water if too thick. Cover, chill until ready to serve. Store in refrigerator up to 3 days.

Salad Dressing

¼ cup sugar
¼ cup white vinegar
⅓ cup ketchup

½ cup vegetable oil
½ cup lemon juice
Onion juice to taste

Whisk together all ingredients.

Honey Mustard Dressing

1 cup olive oil
¼ cup cider vinegar
1⅛ cups honey

¼ cup Dijon mustard
¾ cup mayonnaise
Generous dash garlic salt

Whisk together all ingredients until mayonnaise can't be seen. Chill several hours before serving.

Orange Julius

½ (6-ounce) can orange juice
½ cup milk
1 cup ice water

1 tablespoon sugar
½ teaspoon vanilla extract
5-6 ice cubes

Process all ingredients in a blender until smooth.

Cranberry Bracer

1 (16-ounce) can whole-berry cranberry sauce
1 (8-ounce) container vanilla yogurt

1 cup vanilla ice cream, softened
¼ teaspoon ground cinnamon
⅛ teaspoon ground nutmeg
6 ice cubes

Process all ingredients in a blender until smooth.

Hot Spiced Punch

9	cups pineapple juice	4½	teaspoons whole cloves
9	cups cranberry-apple juice	4	(3-inch) cinnamon sticks
4½	cups water		Pinch of salt
1	cup brown sugar		

Combine first 3 ingredients in pitcher of a coffee pot. Combine sugar and remaining ingredients, and place in filter basket. Brew as directed.

Hot Cider Punch

4	cups water	⅛	teaspoon ground nutmeg
4	cups apple juice	⅛	teaspoon ground cloves
1	cup presweetened powdered fruit drink mix (any flavor)	⅛	teaspoon ground cinnamon

Combine water and apple juice in a saucepan. Add remaining ingredients, stirring well. Bring just to a boil. Serve hot.

Peach Fizz

1	(6-ounce) can frozen limeade concentrate	2	tablespoons lime juice
1	small box peach gelatin	1	(20-ounce) bottle tonic water, chilled
1	(29-ounce) can sliced peaches, undrained		Lime slices for garnish

Prepare limeade in a 3-quart pitcher. Remove 1 cup limeade to a 1-quart saucepan. Bring to a boil over high heat. Remove from heat; stir in gelatin until dissolved. Stir mixture into remaining limeade in pitcher. Process half of peaches and syrup in a blender until smooth. Repeat with remaining peaches and syrup. Stir peach purée and lime juice into limeade mixture. Chill at least 1 hour or until well chilled. To serve, stir tonic water into limeade mixture. Garnish with lime slices.

Wassail Bowl

2	quarts apple cider or juice	1	(6-ounce) can frozen orange juice concentrate
3	(3-inch) cinnamon sticks	1	(6-ounce) can frozen lemonade concentrate
2	teaspoons whole allspice	1	(750 ml) bottle dry white wine
2	teaspoons whole cloves	4	cups water
1	small orange, sliced	¾	cup packed brown sugar
1	small lemon, sliced		

Bring first 4 ingredients to a boil in a 5-quart saucepan over high heat. Reduce heat to low; cover and simmer 15 minutes. Place orange and lemon slices in a heat-safe 5-quart punch bowl; set aside. Add orange juice and lemonade concentrates, wine, water, and sugar. Bring mixture to a boil over high heat. Pour over fruit in bowl.

Party Punch

1	small can fruit punch	1	can frozen lemonade concentrate
1	large can orange juice	1	bottle ginger ale
1	large can pineapple juice		Sherbet or ice cream
1	can frozen orange juice concentrate		

Combine first 6 ingredients in a punch bowl. Add scoops of ice cream, and serve.

Vegetables

Denise Johnson
Kidney transplant recipient,
2007

After a long battle with end-stage renal disease, including three years of dialysis, Denise received her kidney transplant in November 2007.

Corn Pudding

1	cup seasoned grits	1	teaspoon vanilla extract
1	can whole kernel corn	½	teaspoon ground cinnamon
1	can cream-style corn		Dash of salt
¼	cup sugar	2	eggs
1	stick butter or margarine, melted	½	cup milk

Combine first 8 ingredients. Beat eggs and milk; fold into corn mixture. Pour in a lightly greased baking dish. Bake at 325° to 350° or until lightly browned.

Eggplant Casserole

1	eggplant, peeled and cut into chunks	1	onion, chopped
1	(16-ounce) can tomatoes, chopped	2	celery stalks, chopped
		1	beef bouillon cube
			Shredded cheese

Bring eggplant and water to cover to a boil in a saucepan. Cook until tender; drain and remove from saucepan. Combine tomatoes and next 3 ingredients in saucepan; simmer, stirring often, until blended. Add eggplant to tomato mixture, and pour into a baking dish. Bake at 350° for 30 minutes; top with cheese, and bake 5 more minutes or until cheese melts.

Candied Sweet Potatoes

3	cups mashed sweet potato	½	cup milk
1	cup butter or margarine, softened	1	cup chopped pecans
1	cup sugar	⅓	cup butter or margarine
1	tablespoon vanilla extract	⅓	cup all-purpose flour
2	eggs	1	cup firmly packed brown sugar

Beat first 6 ingredients at medium speed with an electric mixer until blended. Pour into a baking dish. Combine pecans and next 3 ingredients; sprinkle over potato mixture. Bake at 350° for 30 minutes.

Italian Spinach

1	package frozen chopped spinach	2	tablespoons grated Parmesan cheese
2	tablespoons olive oil		Garlic powder to taste
		1	egg, lightly beaten

Cook spinach according to package directions; drain well, pressing between paper towels to remove excess moisture. Heat oil in a skillet over medium heat. Add spinach, cheese, and garlic powder, stirring until blended. Stir in egg, and cook thoroughly (about 4 minutes).

Easy Baked Potatoes

5	medium-sized red potatoes, peeled	1	tablespoon Worcestershire sauce
1	can cream of mushroom soup	½	cup milk
			Pepper to taste

Cut potatoes into ¼-inch-thick slices; arrange in rows, overlapping, in a lightly greased 13- x 9-inch pan. Combine soup and remaining ingredients, and pour over potato slices. Bake at 350° for 40 to 45 minutes or until lightly browned.

Squash Medley

1	cup sliced celery		Salt to taste
½	medium-size green bell pepper, cut into ¼-inch strips	½	teaspoon ground ginger
1	small onion, sliced	1½	cups sliced yellow squash
1	tablespoon butter or margarine	2	tomatoes, cut into eighths

Combine first 6 ingredients in a 1½-quart baking dish. Cover tightly, and microwave at HIGH 3 minutes. Stir in squash. Cover tightly, and microwave at HIGH 2 to 4 minutes or until vegetables are crisp-tender. Stir in tomato; cover and microwave at HIGH 2 to 3 minutes.

Squash Casserole

½ cup butter or margarine, melted
1 package cornbread stuffing mix
2 cups yellow squash, cooked and mashed

1 (10¾-ounce) can cream of mushroom soup
1 cup sour cream
2 carrots, grated
1 onion, chopped
1 (2-ounce) jar diced pimiento, drained
Salt and pepper to taste

Combine butter and stuffing mix; place half of mixture in bottom of a baking dish. Combine squash and next 6 ingredients; spoon over stuffing mixture in dish. Top with remaining stuffing mixture. Bake at 350° for 30 minutes.

Macaroni and Cheese

1 package small elbow macaroni
½ (8-ounce) loaf process cheese spread, cubed

1 (5-ounce) can evaporated milk
2 tablespoons milk

Cook pasta according to package directions; drain. Stir in cheese, milk, and butter. Cook over low heat until cheese melts and mixture is thoroughly heated.

Rice Au Gratin

3 cups cooked long-grain rice
1 small onion, chopped
1 small green bell pepper, chopped
1 (4-ounce) jar diced pimiento, drained

1 (10¾-ounce) can cream of mushroom soup
¼ cup milk
½ cup (2 ounces) shredded Cheddar cheese

Combine first 6 ingredients; spoon into a 10- x 6-inch baking dish. Bake at 350° for 40 minutes. Top with cheese, and bake 5 more minutes.

Holiday Baked Corn

2   (16-ounce) cans cream-style corn
¼   cup chopped green bell pepper
¼   cup chopped green onions

2   tablespoons chopped pimiento
4   eggs, lightly beaten
1   tablespoon all-purpose flour
1   teaspoon sugar
    Salt and pepper to taste

Combine all ingredients, and pour into a greased baking dish. Bake at 325° for 1 hour.

Potato Casserole Supreme

1   small package hash browns, thawed
1   small onion, chopped
1   (8-ounce) loaf process cheese spread, shredded

1   (10¾-ounce) can cream of mushroom soup
1   (8-ounce) container sour cream

Combine all ingredients; pour into a baking dish. Bake at 350° for 45 minutes.

Shoepeg Casserole

½   cup chopped celery
½   cup chopped green bell pepper
½   cup chopped onion
1   can French-cut green beans, drained
1   can white shoepeg corn, drained

½   cup (2 ounces) shredded Cheddar cheese
1   (10¾-ounce) can cream of mushroom soup
1   cup sour cream
½   cup butter or margarine, melted
1   tube buttery round crackers, crushed

Combine first 8 ingredients; spoon into a 13- x 8½-inch baking dish. Stir together butter and cracker crumbs; sprinkle over casserole. Bake at 350° for 45 minutes.

Baked Beans

1	pound ground beef	½	box light brown sugar
1	large onion, chopped	1	small bottle ketchup
1	green bell pepper, chopped	1	teaspoon chili powder
1	large can pork and beans		

Cook beef, onion, and bell pepper in a large skillet over medium heat until meat is browned; drain. Stir in pork and beans and next 3 ingredients. Reduce heat, and simmer 1 hour; or place in slow cooker on LOW for 3 to 4 hours.

Asparagus Casserole

2	(14½-ounce) cans asparagus spears	2	cups (8 ounces) shredded Cheddar cheese
2	(10¾-ounce) cans cream of mushroom soup	4	hard-cooked eggs, sliced
2	cups round buttery cracker crumbs	½	cup slivered almonds

Drain asparagus, reserving a small amount of liquid. Stir reserved liquid into soup. Combine cracker crumbs and cheese. Arrange half of asparagus in a 3-quart baking dish; top with half each of soup mixture, cracker crumb mixture, egg slices, and almonds. Repeat procedure. Bake, uncovered, at 350° for 30 minutes.

Bird's Nest Quiche

4	large potatoes	6	eggs
1	egg white, lightly beaten	½	cup milk
1	cup chopped broccoli	1	cup (4 ounces) shredded cheese
1	cup chopped cauliflower		

Cut potatoes into matchsticks. Toss gently with a small amount of flour and the ½ cup milk, and press into a lightly greased 9-inch pie plate. Coat potato with egg white. Bake at 350° until lightly browned. Combine broccoli and next 4 ingredients. Pour into prepared pie plate. Bake at 350° for 45 minutes.

Spinach Casserole

2	pints spinach, cooked and well drained	½	cup mayonnaise
1	onion, chopped	1	cup (4 ounces) shredded cheese
2	eggs, beaten	4	slices bread, toasted, buttered, and crumbled
1	(10¾-ounce) can cream of mushroom soup		

Combine first 5 ingredients. Spoon into a lightly greased baking dish; bake at 350° for 45 minutes. Top with cheese and breadcrumbs; cook until cheese melts.

Mexican Rice

1	cup uncooked long-grain rice	1	teaspoon salt
2	tablespoons vegetable oil	½	teaspoon ground cumin
1	garlic clove, crushed	⅓	(8-ounce) can tomato sauce
½	small onion, finely grated	2	cups hot water

Sauté rice in hot oil in a skillet over medium heat until golden brown. Add garlic and onion; sauté until onion is transparent. Add salt and next 3 ingredients; bring mixture to a boil. Reduce heat, and simmer, without stirring, 25 to 30 minutes or until rice is cooked and a little dry.

English Pea Casserole

1	small onion, chopped	1	can English peas, drained
2	tablespoons chopped green bell pepper	1	(2-ounce) jar diced pimiento
1	cup sliced celery	1	(10¾-ounce) can cream of mushroom soup
½	cup butter or margarine	½	cup fine, dry breadcrumbs
1	can sliced water chestnuts, undrained		

Sauté first 3 ingredients in ½ cup butter in a medium skillet until tender. Add water chestnuts and liquid, peas, and pimiento. Spoon into a 2-quart baking dish; top with soup. Sprinkle with breadcrumbs. Bake at 350° for 25 to 30 minutes or until bubbly and thoroughly heated.

Sweet Potato Croquettes

2½ cups mashed sweet potato
1½ tablespoons butter or
     margarine
2   tablespoons brown sugar
Salt and pepper to taste
Fine, dry breadcrumbs
1   egg, beaten

Beat sweet potato and next 3 ingredients at medium speed with an electric mixer until fluffy. Chill. Shape mixture into patties. Roll in breadcrumbs; dip into egg. Roll in breadcrumbs again. Deep-fry 3 to 5 minutes. Drain.

Mrs. Walton's Potatoes

5   potatoes, unpeeled
½   cup vegetable oil
1   teaspoon garlic powder
1   teaspoon paprika
1   teaspoon salt
     Parmesan cheese

Cut each potato into 8 wedges. Place in a 13- x 9-inch baking dish. Combine oil and next 3 ingredients, and pour over potato wedges; toss gently to coat. Bake at 375° for 40 minutes, stirring every 15 minutes. Sprinkle mixture with Parmesan cheese, and bake 10 more minutes.

Cheesy Corn

1   large package frozen corn
     kernels, thawed
½   (8-ounce) package cream
     cheese, cubed
4   tablespoons butter or
     margarine
1   can cream-style corn
     (optional)

Combine first 3 ingredients and, if desired, cream-style corn in a large bowl. Microwave on HIGH until warm and creamy, stirring often.

Caramel Sweet Potatoes

4   large sweet potatoes, cooked
     and sliced
1   cup brown sugar
1   cup pecans, chopped
¼   cup butter or margarine
¼   teaspoon ground nutmeg

Spoon potato slices into a baking dish. Combine brown sugar and next 3 ingredients. Sprinkle over potato slices. Bake at 350° for 10 to 15 minutes or until sugar caramelizes.

Green Beans-and-Peas Casserole

2 cans green beans, undrained	⅓ can milk
1 can English peas, drained	1 (8-ounce) jar process cheese
1 medium onion	spread
1 (10¾-ounce) can cream of	Fine, dry breadcrumbs
mushroom soup	

Bring green beans and liquid to a boil in a large saucepan; drain. Alternate layers of beans and peas in a baking dish. Cook onion, soup, and milk in a saucepan over medium heat until thoroughly heated. Add cheese, stirring until it melts. Pour soup mixture over beans mixture. Top with breadcrumbs. Bake at 350° for 30 to 35 minutes.

Mixed Veggie Casserole

1 cup chopped onion	1½ cups (6 ounces) shredded
1 cup chopped celery	Cheddar cheese
2 cans mixed vegetables, drained	½ cup butter or margarine, melted
1 can sliced water chestnuts, drained	1 tube round buttery crackers, crushed
1 cup mayonnaise	

Sauté onion and celery in a nonstick skillet. Add mixed vegetables and next 3 ingredients. Pour mixture into a 13- x 9-inch baking dish. Stir together melted butter and cracker crumbs. Sprinkle over casserole. Bake at 350° for 30 minutes.

Broccoli-Corn Casserole

1 egg, lightly beaten	Salt and pepper to taste
1 (10-ounce) package frozen chopped broccoli, partially thawed	3 tablespoons melted butter or margarine
1 can cream-style corn	1 cup herb-seasoned stuffing mix
1 tablespoon grated onion	

Combine first 5 ingredients in a bowl. Stir together butter and stuffing mix. Add ¾ cup stuffing mixture to corn mixture. Pour into a 1-quart baking dish. Sprinkle with remaining ¼ cup stuffing mixture. Bake, uncovered, at 350° for 35 minutes.

Good Gosh Beans

1	pound ground beef	2	teaspoons cayenne pepper
2	large cans baked beans	⅓	cup dark molasses
1	garlic clove, pressed	2	jalapeño peppers, chopped
1	large onion, finely chopped	1	can whole kernel corn
1	cup hickory-flavored barbecue	1	cup beer
	sauce	1	teaspoon ground ginger
	Dash of Worcestershire sauce	4	potatoes, cubed
1	teaspoon dry mustard		

Brown beef in a skillet over medium heat; drain. Place beef and remaining ingredients in a slow cooker. Cook on HIGH 2 hours; reduce setting to LOW, and cook 2 to 4 hours or until ready to serve.

Gloria's Macaroni

4	cups cooked elbow macaroni	1½	teaspoons salt
½	cup chopped onion	2	tablespoons dried parsley
1	cup mayonnaise		flakes
1½	cups chopped celery	2	teaspoons white vinegar or
1½	cups frozen English peas,		lemon juice
	thawed	½	teaspoon celery seed
1	cup chopped green bell	⅛	teaspoon pepper
	pepper	2	teaspoons prepared mustard
1	(2¼-ounce) can sliced ripe		Pinch of sugar
	olives		Paprika

Stir together first 14 ingredients in a serving dish; sprinkle with paprika. Store in refrigerator.

Scalloped Potatoes

5	potatoes, sliced	½	cup butter or margarine,
	Cheddar cheese, cubed		cubed
1	pound bacon, diced	1	cup evaporated milk
			Salt and pepper to taste

Line a baking dish with potato slices. Sprinkle evenly with cheese and bacon; dot with butter. Scatter milk over top. Repeat procedure until potato slices are used, ending with cheese-and-bacon layer. Bake at 350° for 45 minutes or until potato is tender.

Bolitos
(Mexican Stuffed Potatoes)

8	large potatoes	Shredded romaine lettuce
2	avocados	Shredded Monterey Jack or
	Salt to taste	Cheddar cheese
1	tablespoon butter or	Diced tomato
	margarine	Diced jalapeño
1	large onion, sliced	Sour cream or plain yogurt
1	cup sliced fresh mushrooms	Fresh Salsa

Bake potatoes at 500° for 50 minutes. Mash avocados, adding a little water and salt to taste. Melt butter in a small skillet; sauté onion and mushrooms in butter until tender. Cut each potato in half, and top with avocado mixture, onion mixture, lettuce, and next 5 ingredients.

Fresh Salsa

2	large ripe tomatoes, finely chopped	3	tablespoons chopped fresh cilantro
2	green onions, thinly sliced		Finely chopped jalapeño pepper to taste

Combine first 3 ingredients; add jalapeño to taste.

Oven Rice Pilaf

2	tablespoons butter or margarine	4	cups boiling water
1	large onion, diced	1	tablespoon dried parsley flakes
1½	cups uncooked rice	¼	teaspoon garlic powder
½	cup chopped mushrooms	¼	teaspoon pepper
5	chicken bouillon cubes		

Melt butter in a skillet over low heat. Add onion, rice, and mushrooms. Sauté until onion is tender and rice begins to brown. Remove from heat, and spoon mixture into a greased 2-quart casserole. Dissolve bouillon cubes in boiling water. Pour over rice mixture. Stir in parsley, garlic powder, and pepper. Bake, covered, at 350° for 1 hour or until rice is tender and liquid is absorbed.

Creamy Potatoes

2 pounds frozen hash browns, thawed
2 (10¾-ounce) cans cream of potato soup
1 (10¾-ounce) can cream of celery soup
1 (10¾-ounce) can Cheddar cheese soup
½ cup milk

Combine all ingredients, and pour into a greased 13- x 9-inch baking dish. Bake, uncovered, at 325° for 1 hour and 20 minutes.

Potato Puffs

6 baking potatoes, grated
2 eggs, beaten
   Salt and pepper to taste
½ teaspoon baking powder
7 tablespoons all-purpose flour
   Minced onion to taste
   Vegetable oil

Combine first 6 ingredients, and set aside. Heat oil in a large skillet over medium-high heat. Drop potato mixture by tablespoonfuls into hot oil. Flatten with a spatula, and cook until browned on both sides.

Baked Beans

2 large cans pork and beans
1 pound bacon slices
1 large onion, diced
1 cup packed brown sugar
1 bottle ketchup
2 tablespoons prepared mustard or 1 teaspoon dry mustard

Combine all ingredients. Spoon into a baking dish. Bake at 350° for 30 minutes; reduce temperature to 275°, and bake 3½ more hours.

Potatoes Romanov

1 cup (4 ounces) shredded Cheddar cheese, divided
6 medium potatoes, cooked and mashed
¼ medium onion, grated
1 cup sour cream
   Salt and pepper to taste

Combine ½ cup cheese and remaining ingredients, and pour into a lightly greased baking dish. Sprinkle with remaining cheese. Bake at 350° for 30 minutes.

Squash Casserole

1 medium onion, chopped
½ cup butter or margarine, melted
2 cups cooked yellow squash
1 (10¾-ounce) can cream of mushroom soup
⅔ cup evaporated milk
1 cup crushed round buttery crackers

1 cup (4 ounces) shredded Cheddar cheese
Salt to taste
½ cup crushed round buttery crackers
½ cup (2 ounces) shredded Cheddar cheese

Combine onion and butter in a small bowl. Microwave at HIGH 3 to 4 minutes or until onion is transparent. Combine next 6 ingredients; stir in onion mixture. Pour into a 2-quart baking dish. Bake, uncovered, at 350° for 30 minutes. Sprinkle with ½ cup cracker crumbs and ½ cup cheese. Bake 10 more minutes.

Southern Sweet Potato Casserole

3 cups mashed sweet potato
½ cup sugar
¼ cup butter or margarine, melted
2 eggs, beaten
1 teaspoon vanilla extract
½ teaspoon orange extract

¼ cup milk
½ teaspoon ground cinnamon
½ teaspoon ground ginger
1 cup packed light brown sugar
¼ cup all-purpose flour
⅓ cup soft margarine
¾ cup chopped pecans

Combine first 9 ingredients. Spoon into a greased 3-quart baking dish. Bake at 350° for 25 to 30 minutes. Combine brown sugar and next 3 ingredients; sprinkle over casserole. Bake 15 more minutes.

Make-Ahead Potatoes

5 pounds baking potatoes, peeled
2 (3-ounce) packages cream cheese, softened
1 cup sour cream

2 teaspoons chopped onion
¼ teaspoon salt
¼ teaspoon pepper
1 tablespoon butter or margarine

Cook potatoes in boiling water to cover until tender. Mash potatoes. Add remaining ingredients; beat at medium speed with an electric mixer until fluffy. Spoon into a greased baking dish. Cover and chill at least 24 hours. Bake at 350° for 35 to 45 minutes.

Main Dishes

Danielle Arnold
Kidney transplant recipient,
2007

Danielle, left, was all smiles with her organ donor, Cat Ramos, before the surgery that changed her life. Cat generously donated a kidney to Danielle, who battled diabetes for years and was eventually diagnosed with end-stage renal failure.

Danielle received her lifesaving transplant in October 2007. Both women have fully recovered and are doing well today.

Stir-Fried Pork Tenderloin With Vegetables

¾ pound pork tenderloin	½ bunch broccoli, chopped
3 tablespoons soy sauce	1 (8-ounce) package sliced fresh
1 tablespoon dry sherry	mushrooms
2½ teaspoons cornstarch	1 carrot, thinly sliced
1¼ teaspoons sugar	¼ teaspoon salt
¼ teaspoon minced fresh ginger	2 tablespoons water
Vegetable oil	

With knife held in slanted position, almost parallel to cutting surface, cut tenderloin crosswise into ⅛-inch-thick slices. Combine pork and next 5 ingredients in a medium bowl; set aside. Stir-fry broccoli and next 3 ingredients in 3 tablespoons hot oil over high heat in a 12-inch skillet or wok until vegetables are coated with oil. Add water, and stir-fry until crisp-tender. Spoon onto a warm serving plate. Add 2 tablespoons oil to skillet; stir-fry pork mixture in hot oil 2 to 3 minutes or until pork is no longer pink in center. Return vegetables to skillet; stir-fry until thoroughly heated.

Stuffed Potatoes With Italian Sausage

4 baking potatoes	2 tablespoons dried parsley
½ pound Italian sausage	flakes
2 tablespoons butter or	Salt and pepper to taste
margarine	½ pound diced mozzarella
2 tablespoons shredded cheese	cheese
Milk	

Bake potatoes at 400° for 45 minutes or until tender. Cut in half lengthwise. Cook sausage according to package directions; remove casings, and mince. Scoop pulp from potato halves into a large bowl, reserving potato shells. Add butter, 2 tablespoons cheese, and enough milk to potato pulp to mash until smooth. Stir in sausage, parsley, salt, and pepper. Spoon sausage mixture into potato shells, and sprinkle with mozzarella; place on a baking sheet. Bake at 350° until thoroughly heated and mozzarella melts.

Spicy Cranberry Pork Chops

4	pork loin chops	2	tablespoons red wine vinegar
	Salt and pepper	2	tablespoons orange juice
8	ounces whole-berry cranberry sauce	½	teaspoon ground cinnamon
¼	cup raisins	½	teaspoon grated orange rind
2	tablespoons brown sugar	½	teaspoon salt

Sprinkle chops with salt and pepper. Place in a 13- x 9-inch baking dish. Cover with plastic wrap; microwave at MEDIUM-LOW (30 percent power) 16 minutes, turning chops and rotating dish a half turn after 10 minutes.

Combine cranberry sauce and next 7 ingredients in a small bowl. Drain liquid from chops; spoon cranberry mixture over chops. Cover with plastic wrap, and microwave at MEDIUM-LOW 6 to 8 minutes or until chops are no longer pink inside.

Cheesy Potatoes With Ham

1	tablespoon butter or margarine	1	cup milk
2	tablespoons all-purpose flour	½	cup (2 ounces) shredded Cheddar cheese
1	teaspoon salt	2	cups diced potato
1	teaspoon pepper	1	cup diced cooked ham

Melt butter in a skillet over low heat. Stir in flour, salt, and pepper. Gradually stir in milk; cook, stirring constantly, until mixture thickens. Remove from heat, and stir in cheese. Alternate layers of potato and ham in a greased baking dish. Pour milk mixture over top. Bake, covered, at 375° for 30 minutes. Uncover and bake 10 more minutes.

Home-Style Dressing

¼	cup butter or margarine	2	cans condensed chicken broth
1	cup mushrooms	1	(16-ounce) package herb-seasoned stuffing mix
1	cup chopped onion		
1	cup chopped celery		

Melt butter in a 4-quart saucepan over medium heat. Sauté mushrooms, onion, and celery until tender. Add broth, and bring to a boil. Add stuffing mix, stirring until moistened. Spoon into a 13- x 9-inch baking dish. Bake, covered, at 350° for 20 minutes. Uncover and bake 10 more minutes.

Glazed Barbecued Brisket

1 (4-pound) beef brisket	Apple-Mustard Glaze or
Water	Apricot Glaze*
Honey-and-Spice Glaze or	

Bring brisket and water to cover to a boil in an 8-quart saucepan. Reduce heat, and simmer 2 to 2½ hours or until beef is tender. Remove to a plate, and chill until ready to grill. Grill beef over medium-low heat 30 minutes or until thoroughly heated, basting with glaze and turning occasionally.

To bake in oven, place cooked brisket in a 13- x 9-inch baking dish. Bake at 325° for 45 minutes or until thoroughly heated, basting occasionally with glaze.

*Recipes for glazes can be found in the back of this section.

Sausage and Peppers

6 links Italian sausage	½ cup red bell pepper strips
¼ cup water	¼ teaspoon dried basil
1 cup sliced onion	¼ teaspoon garlic powder
½ cup green bell pepper strips	

Place sausage and water in a skillet; cook, covered, over medium-low heat 15 minutes. Uncover and bring to a boil; cook until water evaporates. Remove casings from sausage, and cut into 2-inch pieces. Combine sausage, onion, and remaining ingredients In skillet. Cook over medium heat until vegetables are tender. Serve with pasta.

Round Steak With Rich Gravy

½ cup all-purpose flour	1 (10¾-ounce) can cream of
3 pounds round steak	mushroom soup
3 tablespoons shortening	½ cup water
1 (1-ounce) envelope dry onion	
soup mix	

Pound flour into steak. Cut steak into serving pieces. Brown steak in shortening in a large skillet. Sprinkle soup mix over steak. Combine mushroom soup and ½ cup water; pour over steak mixture. Cover and simmer 1½ to 2 hours. Remove steak to a serving plate. Bring sauce mixture to boil, stirring constantly. Pour over steak.

Fried Rice

2	tablespoons vegetable oil	2	cups diced cooked pork steak
4	cups white rice		(or chicken or beef)
4	tablespoons garlic powder	½	cup cooked, crumbled bacon
1	bunch green onions, chopped	3	teaspoons salt
6	eggs, scrambled	1	teaspoon paprika
		1	cup soy sauce

Heat oil in an 8-quart stockpot over medium-high heat. Add rice, and sauté until light brown. Stir in garlic powder; remove from heat, and cool slightly. Add enough water to cover rice mixture. Bring to a boil; reduce heat, and simmer 35 to 40 minutes. In a small skillet, sauté green onions until tender. Add green onions and next 5 ingredients to rice mixture. Cook until rice is tender. Stir in soy sauce.

Corned Beef Hash Rolls

1	(15-ounce) can corned beef hash	¼	teaspoon pepper
		⅓	cup ketchup
1	tablespoon Worcestershire sauce	2½	cups self-rising flour
		⅓	cup shortening
¼	teaspoon salt	1	cup milk

Combine first 5 ingredients. Set aside. Place flour in a bowl; cut in shortening with a pastry blender until mixture is crumbly. Add milk, and stir well. Turn mixture out onto a lightly floured surface, and knead until a soft dough forms. Roll into a thin sheet. Spread with corned beef mixture. Roll up dough, jelly roll fashion. Slice into ½-inch slices, and place on cookie sheets. Bake at 400° for 20 minutes or until browned.

Mama's Frosted Meat Loaf

1½	pounds ground beef	½	teaspoon salt
1	can golden mushroom soup		Dash of pepper
1	cup small white bread cubes	2	cups mashed potato
¼	cup finely chopped onion	¼	cup water
1	egg, lightly beaten		

Combine beef, ½ cup soup, and next 5 ingredients. Shape firmly into a loaf. Place in a shallow baking dish. Bake at 350° for 1 hour. Spread loaf with mashed potato. Bake 15 more minutes. Stir together remaining soup, water, and 2 tablespoons pan drippings. Heat and serve with loaf.

Cajun Crawfish/Shrimp Étouffé

½	cup butter or margarine	3	medium tomatoes, peeled, seeded, and chopped
1	medium onion, chopped		
1	bunch green onions, sliced	2	pounds medium-size fresh shrimp or crawfish, peeled
1	medium green bell pepper, chopped		
2	garlic cloves, minced	2	(6-ounce) cans tomato paste
3	celery stalks, chopped	¼	cup dry sherry
		6	dashes hot sauce
			Salt to taste

Melt butter in a large Dutch oven over medium heat; add onion and next 4 ingredients, and sauté 15 minutes. Add tomato. Cook, stirring occasionally, 15 minutes. Add shrimp and remaining ingredients, and simmer 20 to 30 minutes. Serve over rice or pasta.

Ham-Broccoli Bake

3	cups self-rising flour	½	teaspoon salt
1	can Cheddar cheese soup	½	teaspoon pepper
¾	cup milk	1	teaspoon prepared horseradish
2	cups chopped cooked ham		
⅓	cup chopped onion	1	(10-ounce) package frozen chopped broccoli, thawed
1	can mushroom pieces		
½	cup milk		

Combine flour, ½ can soup, and ¾ cup milk to form a soft dough. Pat into a greased 13- x 9-inch baking dish. Spread ham, onion, and mushrooms over dough. Combine remaining ½ can soup, ½ cup milk, and next 3 ingredients; pour over mushrooms. Top with broccoli. Bake at 350° for 30 minutes.

Stuffed Cabbage

1	pound ground beef	¼	teaspoon salt
½	pound ground pork sausage	2	eggs, lightly beaten
¼	cup chopped onion	2	cups tomato sauce, divided
¼	teaspoon pepper	1	large cabbage

Combine first 6 ingredients and 1 cup tomato sauce. Remove core from cabbage; simmer in water to cover until leaves are wilted. Remove and run under cold water. Spoon ¼ cup meat mixture on a large cabbage leaf; roll up, and secure with a wooden pick. Repeat procedure until meat mixture is used. Place rolls in a baking dish. Spread with remaining tomato sauce. Bake, covered, at 350° 1 hour or until tender.

Green Bell Pepper Steak

1	pound beef round steak	1	cup red or green bell pepper
¼	cup soy sauce		squares
1	garlic clove, pressed	2	stalks celery, thinly sliced
½	teaspoon minced fresh ginger	1	tablespoon cornstarch
	or 1 teaspoon ground ginger	1	cup water
¼	cup vegetable oil	2	tomatoes, cut into wedges
1	cup thinly sliced green onions		

Cut beef across the grain into ⅛-inch-thick strips; place in a bowl. Combine soy sauce, garlic, and ginger; pour over beef, tossing to coat. Stir-fry beef in hot oil in a skillet or wok over high heat until browned. If beef isn't tender, cover and simmer 30 to 40 minutes. Return heat to high, and add onions, bell pepper, and celery. Stir-fry 10 minutes or until vegetables are tender. Combine cornstarch and water; stir into skillet, and cook until mixture thickens. Add tomato wedges, and cook until thoroughly heated.

You may prepare the beef ahead and chill.

Greek Venison Stew

3	pounds boneless venison	1	(14-ounce) can stewed
1	cup vinegar		tomatoes
1	cup water	1	cup dry red wine
	Juice of 2 lemons	1	teaspoon ground allspice
1	bay leaf, crushed	1	teaspoon pickling spice
12	whole cloves	1	bay leaf
½	cup vegetable oil	3	teaspoons salt
5	garlic cloves, pressed	¼	teaspoon pepper
3	tablespoons tomato paste	5	pounds small whole onions, peeled

Cut venison into 1½-inch cubes, and place in a deep bowl. Combine vinegar and next 4 ingredients; toss with venison. Cover and chill 1 to 2 days, turning meat often. Drain, discarding marinade. Brown meat in hot oil in a large Dutch oven. Add pressed garlic and next 8 ingredients. Cover and simmer 1½ hours. Place onions over meat, and cook ½ hour or until meat is tender and liquid is reduced. Add water only if necessary. Serve with wild rice.

Hamburger Pie

1	pound ground beef	1	can mixed peas and carrots, undrained
2	tablespoons butter or margarine	2	beef bouillon cubes
⅓	cup diced onion	1	cup diced cooked potato (optional)
⅓	tablespoon salt		
	Dash of pepper	⅓	cup all-purpose flour
	Dash of garlic powder	1	(15-ounce) package refrigerated piecrusts
¼	cup diced green bell pepper		

Brown beef in butter over medium heat in a large skillet; drain. Add onion and next 4 ingredients. Cook until thoroughly heated. Add peas and carrots, bouillon cubes, and, if desired, potato; cook until bouillon dissolves. Stir in flour to thicken. Fit 1 piecrust into a pie plate. Pour beef mixture into crust. Top with remaining crust; fold edges under, and crimp. Bake at 400° for 20 to 25 minutes. Serve with broiled peaches.

Easy Chili

1	pound ground beef	2	cans tomato sauce
⅓	cup chopped green bell pepper	1	can kidney beans, undrained
1	onion, chopped	1	cup water
		1	envelope chili seasoning mix

Brown beef in a skillet over medium heat; drain. Add bell pepper and onion, and cook until vegetables are crisp-tender. Stir in tomato sauce and remaining ingredients. Reduce heat, cover, and simmer 45 minutes.

Chicken Fajitas

1	whole chicken		Garlic powder
¾	cup butter or margarine	3	medium onions, sliced
1	cup wine	3	green bell peppers, sliced
1	package large flour tortillas	1	block mozzarella cheese, shredded
	Salt and pepper		

Boil chicken. Remove meat from bone, and cube. Melt butter in a skillet; add onion, bell pepper, wine, and spices; sauté until tender. Add chicken. Simmer until liquid is absorbed. Place a small amount of mixture in a warm tortilla. Top with cheese and picante sauce. Roll up.

Chicken Enchiladas

1½ pounds skinned and boned chicken breast halves, cubed
1 envelope taco seasoning mix
½ cup water
½ cup plus 1 tablespoon vegetable oil

12 corn tortillas
2 cans chili with beans
1 (8-ounce) package Monterey Jack cheese, shredded

Sauté chicken in a skillet in 1 tablespoon hot oil until no longer pink. Add taco seasoning and water; simmer until thickened. Pour ½ cup oil in a heavy skillet over low heat. Dip tortillas in hot oil, 1 at a time, until soft enough to roll (5 to 10 seconds). Roll chicken in tortillas, and place in a 13- x 9-inch baking dish. Pour heated chili over enchiladas; sprinkle with cheese. Bake at 350° for 20 minutes or until cheese melts.

Honey Mustard Chicken

1 (20-ounce) can pineapple slices, undrained
4 skinned and boned chicken breast halves
Salt and pepper
2 garlic cloves, pressed

1 teaspoon dried thyme, crumbled
3 teaspoons vegetable oil
1 teaspoon cornstarch
¼ cup honey
¼ cup Dijon mustard

Drain pineapple, reserving juice. Sprinkle chicken with salt and pepper. Rub with garlic and thyme. Brown chicken in hot oil in a nonstick skillet. Combine 2 tablespoons reserved juice with cornstarch; set aside. Combine honey and mustard; stir honey mixture into skillet with remaining juice. Spoon sauce mixture over chicken. Cover and simmer 15 minutes. Stir cornstarch mixture into pan juices. Add pineapple slices, and cook, stirring constantly, until sauce boils and thickens.

Oriental Chicken

Soy sauce
1 ginger root, grated
Sesame oil (optional)

2 pounds boneless chicken breast, cubed
All-purpose flour
Vegetable oil

Combine soy sauce, ginger, and, if desired, sesame oil in a bowl. Mix well. Add chicken, and chill 2 hours. Drain. Toss chicken with flour; cook in a skillet over medium heat in hot vegetable oil until golden brown.

Chicken Fried Rice

1	pound boneless chicken breast, cubed	2	green onions, sliced
	Butter or vegetable oil	3	cups cold cooked rice
1	carrot, chopped	2	eggs, scrambled
1	green bell pepper, chopped		Soy sauce
1	onion, chopped		Salt and pepper
			Wine (optional)

Sauté chicken in butter in a skillet over medium heat until no longer pink. Add chopped vegetables to chicken. Stir in rice and eggs. Add soy sauce, salt and pepper, and, if desired, wine.

Yakitori

1	container chicken livers	½	cup soy sauce
1	package breast of chicken	¼	cup sake
1	bunch green onions, cut into 1-inch lengths	1	teaspoon pressed garlic
¼	cup mirin (rice) wine	1	teaspoon onion powder

Cut livers and chicken breast into 1-inch pieces. Alternate green onions and livers on skewers. Repeat procedure with green onions and chicken breast. Combine wine and next 4 ingredients in a shallow dish. Place skewers in mixture, turning to coat; chill 30 minutes. Pour marinade into a small saucepan. Bring to a boil. Cook skewers on a griddle 5 to 6 minutes on each side, basting with marinade. Serve over rice.

Mexican Chicken

1	cup crushed tortilla chips	1	cup (4 ounces) shredded Cheddar cheese
4	skinned and boned chicken breast halves, cut into strips	1	tablespoon chili powder
2	(10¾-ounce) cans cream of chicken soup	1	tablespoon garlic powder
1	can tomatoes and chiles	1	cup finely chopped onion
		1	cup chopped green bell pepper

Spread ½ cup crushed chips in a greased (9-inch) cakepan. Arrange chicken over chips. Combine soup, tomatoes and chiles, ½ cup cheese, and next 4 ingredients. Pour mixture over chicken. Bake at 350° for 30 minutes. Sprinkle with remaining ½ cup chips and ½ cup cheese. Bake 7 more minutes.

Planter's Chicken

2	tablespoons butter or margarine	1	small onion, diced
1	baked or boiled potato, diced	4	whole fresh mushrooms, diced
½	green bell pepper, diced	1	whole boneless chicken breast, roasted
1	cooked ham slice, diced		

Melt butter in a large skillet over medium heat. Add potato and next 4 ingredients; sauté until tender. Place on a warm plate; top with chicken. Top 1 side with Hollandaise sauce and 1 side with mushroom sauce.

Chicken Surprise

1	cup butter or margarine	1	(4½-ounce) jar pimiento-stuffed olives, sliced
1	bunch green onions, sliced		
2	(10¾-ounce) cans cream of mushroom soup	3	cups chopped cooked chicken
		12	ounces thin spaghetti, cooked
2	rolls garlic cheese	1	(3-ounce) chow mein noodles

Melt butter in a skillet over medium heat. Sauté onions until tender. Add soup and cheese; cook until cheese melts. Add olives and chicken. Stir into spaghetti, and pour mixture into a 3-quart baking dish. Bake at 350° for 1 hour. Sprinkle with noodles after 45 minutes.

Mexican Chicken

4	whole chicken breasts	⅔	cup chicken broth
1	(10¾-ounce) can cream of chicken soup		Onion flakes
		1½	cups (6 ounces) shredded Cheddar cheese
1	(10¾-ounce) can cream of mushroom soup	1	package nacho-flavored tortilla chips
1	can tomatoes and chiles		

Cook chicken in boiling water to cover until done. Remove meat from bones. Reserve ⅔ cup broth. Bring soups, tomatoes and chiles, and broth to a boil in a saucepan. Divide remaining ingredients, and layer all twice in a baking dish. Pour soup mixture over top. Bake at 350° for 30 minutes. Let stand 10 minutes before serving.

Chicken Monterey

6	chicken breast halves	½	teaspoon dried rosemary,
	Salt		crushed
2	tablespoons vegetable oil	1	chicken bouillon cube
1	green onion, chopped	1	(9-ounce) package frozen
3	tablespoons all-purpose flour		artichoke hearts, thawed
2	cups milk	1	(9-ounce) package frozen
1	cup water		green beans, thawed
3	tablespoons ketchup		

Rub chicken breasts with ¾ teaspoon salt. Brown chicken in a 12-inch skillet in oil over medium-high heat. Arrange chicken in a 3-quart baking dish. Drain all but 2 tablespoons drippings from skillet. Add green onion to drippings, and sauté until tender. Stir in flour. Gradually stir in milk and water until smooth. Stir in ketchup, rosemary, bouillon, and ¾ teaspoon salt. Cook, stirring constantly, until mixture thickens slightly. Pour over chicken. Bake, covered, at 350° for 30 minutes. Stir in artichoke hearts and green beans. Bake 20 more minutes or until chicken is tender.

Creamed Chicken and Fettuccine

2	whole chicken breasts	1½	cups milk
1	egg	2	tablespoons dry sherry
	All-purpose flour	¼	cup grated Parmesan cheese
	Salt and pepper	6	ounces fettuccine, cooked
	Butter or margarine	1	tablespoon chopped fresh
¼	pound sliced fresh		parsley
	mushrooms		

Cut each chicken breast in half. Beat egg lightly in a small bowl. Combine flour, ½ teaspoon salt, and ⅛ teaspoon pepper on wax paper. Dip chicken in egg; dredge in flour mixture. Melt 2 tablespoons butter in a 10-inch skillet over medium-high heat. Add chicken, and cook 10 minutes or until tender. Remove to a platter; keep warm. Add 2 tablespoons butter to drippings in skillet. Add mushrooms, and cook over medium heat until tender. Stir in 2 tablespoons flour, ½ teaspoon salt, and ⅛ teaspoon pepper. Cook, stirring constantly, 1 minute. Stir in milk and sherry; cook, stirring constantly, until mixture thickens. Stir in cheese until melted. Remove 1 cup sauce. Add pasta to sauce in skillet, tossing to coat. Arrange on platter with chicken. Pour remaining 1 cup sauce over chicken. Sprinkle pasta with parsley.

Chicken-(Or Turkey) and-Rice Soufflé

1 cup cooked rice	¾ cup chicken broth
1½ cups diced cooked chicken	2 eggs, separated
Salt to taste	

Combine chicken and rice in a baking dish. Season with salt; stir in broth. Beat egg yolks well; add to chicken mixture. Beat egg whites, and fold into mixture. Bake at 350° until golden brown.

Chicken Pot Pie

1 (15-ounce) package refrigerated piecrusts	1 can mixed vegetables, drained
3 skinned and boned chicken breast halves, cooked and cubed	1 (10¾-ounce) can cream of chicken soup
	1 (10¾-ounce) can cream of mushroom soup

Fit 1 piecrust into a 9-inch pie plate according to package directions. Combine remaining ingredients, and pour into crust. Top with remaining crust; crimp edges to seal. Make several slits in top crust with a sharp knife. Bake at 375° until golden brown.

Spinach and Linguine

2 (10-ounce) packages frozen chopped spinach, thawed	Salt and pepper to taste
2 eggs, beaten	3 cups (12-ounces) shredded Monterey Jack cheese
1 cup sour cream	¾ pound sliced fresh mushrooms (sauté in 2 tablespoons butter, if desired)
½ cup milk	
4 tablespoons grated Parmesan cheese	1 garlic clove, pressed
4 tablespoons thinly sliced green onions	2 tablespoons dry sherry
	16 ounces linguine, cooked

Cook spinach according to package directions. Drain, squeezing out excess moisture with paper towels. Combine spinach and next 6 ingredients. Add Monterey Jack and next 3 ingredients. Place mixture into an oblong baking dish. Sprinkle with additional Parmesan cheese. Bake, covered, at 350° for 30 minutes or until bubbly. Serve with pasta and sliced tomato.

Beer-Battered Fried Shrimp

½ cup all-purpose flour
½ cup beer
1 teaspoon salt

1½ pounds unpeeled, large fresh
shrimp
Vegetable oil

Combine flour, beer, and salt in a small bowl. Peel and devein shrimp; rinse under cold running water, and pat dry with paper towels. Pour oil into a saucepan to a depth of 2 inches. Heat to 375°. Dip shrimp, 1 at a time, into batter, and drop into hot oil. Fry, turning once, 1 minute or until lightly browned. Drain on paper towels.

Stromboli

1 (¼-ounce) envelope active dry
yeast
1 cup warm water
3 cups all-purpose flour

1 teaspoon salt
Ham slices, salami slices,
pepperoni slices, mozzarella
slices, American cheese slices

Dissolve yeast in warm water; stir in flour and salt. Turn out onto a lightly floured surface, and knead 7 minutes. Let rise in a warm place 2 hours. Divide into 8 balls. Let rest. Roll dough into circles. Fill with desired fillings, and fold in half. Arrange on a lightly greased baking sheet. Bake at 375° for 15 to 20 minutes.

Baked Spaghetti

1½ pounds ground beef
1 cup chopped onion
1 garlic clove, pressed
1 (28-ounce) can tomatoes, cut
up
1 (15-ounce) can tomato sauce
1 (4-ounce) can mushroom
pieces, drained
2 teaspoons sugar

1½ teaspoons dried oregano,
crushed
1 teaspoon salt
8 ounces spaghetti, broken and
cooked
2 cups (8 ounces) shredded
mozzarella cheese
⅓ cup grated Parmesan cheese

Brown ground beef in a Dutch oven over medium heat; drain. Add onion and garlic, and sauté until tender. Add tomatoes, tomato sauce, mushrooms, sugar, oregano, and salt. Bring mixture to a boil. Boil, uncovered, 20 to 25 minutes. Remove from heat. Stir in spaghetti. Place half of mixture in a 13- x 9-inch baking dish. Sprinkle with mozzarella. Top with remaining half of spaghetti mixture. Sprinkle with Parmesan. Bake at 375° for 30 minutes.

Annie's Spaghetti

1½ pounds ground beef
1 can tomato soup
1 (8-ounce) can tomato sauce
1 (6-ounce) can tomato paste
2 small cans mushroom pieces
1 teaspoon dried oregano
1 garlic clove, pressed

1 small onion, chopped
1 small green bell pepper, chopped
1 teaspoon chili powder
Salt to taste
1 bay leaf
1½ cups water

Brown beef in a large Dutch oven over medium heat. Drain. Add remaining ingredients; reduce heat, and simmer 2 hours. Remove and discard bay leaf.

Manicotti

2 pounds ricotta cheese
½ pound mozzarella cheese, shredded
2 eggs, well beaten
2 tablespoons chopped fresh parsley

½ teaspoon pepper
1 teaspoon salt
1 cup grated Parmesan cheese
1 large package manicotti noodles

Use about 30 ounces sauce (homemade or from a jar) for this recipe. Combine ricotta and next 6 ingredients. Stuff into uncooked manicotti noodles. Pour one-third sauce into a 13- x 11-inch pan. Arrange manicotti over sauce. Pour remaining sauce over top. Sprinkle with additional Parmesan cheese, if desired. Cover with aluminum foil. Bake at 350° for 1 hour.

Pork Chop Casserole

6 pork chops
1 large onion, chopped
2 garlic cloves, pressed
Salt and pepper to taste

5 large potatoes, peeled and cut as for French fries
2 cups tomato sauce
2 cups water

Place pork chops in a baking dish. Top with onion, garlic, salt, pepper, and potato. Combine tomato sauce and water, and pour over vegetables. Bake at 400° for 1 hour or until chops are tender.

Taco Casserole

¼   cup butter or margarine
1   whole white onion, chopped
1   green bell pepper, chopped
1½ pounds ground chuck
1   small package medium egg
     noodles, cooked

2   cans Mexican-style corn
2   cans cream of tomato soup
2   cups broken nacho-flavored
     tortilla chips

Melt butter in a skillet over medium heat. Add onion and bell pepper, and sauté until tender. Set aside. Brown beef in skillet over medium heat. Drain. Add noodles to skillet with beef. Add onion mixture, corn, and soup to beef mixture. Sprinkle ¼ cup broken chips into bottom of a 13- x 9-inch baking dish. Stir remaining chips into beef mixture. Pour over chips in dish. Bake at 350° for 30 minutes.

Enchilada Casserole

2   pounds ground beef
1   onion, chopped
1   (4.5-ounce) can chopped
     green chiles
1   tablespoon chili powder
1   (10¾-ounce) can cream of
     mushroom soup

1   (10¾-ounce) can cream of
     chicken soup
1   large can evaporated milk
1   bag tortilla chips
1   cup (4-ounces) shredded
     Cheddar cheese

Brown beef in a skillet over medium heat; drain. Add onion and chiles, and sauté until tender. Stir In chili powder. Add soups and milk. Cover bottom of a greased 2-quart baking dish with broken tortilla chips. Pour beef mixture over chips. Sprinkle with cheese. Bake at 350° for 40 minutes.

Smoked Sausage Casserole

1   package smoked sausage
1   small onion, chopped and
     sautéed

6   medium potatoes, peeled and
     cut into chunks
1   can green beans
     Salt and pepper to taste

Cut sausage into 1-inch pieces in a large bowl. Add onion, potato, and green beans. Stir in 1 can water and seasonings. Place in a baking dish. Bake at 350° for about 45 minutes.

Cornbread Chicken Casserole

¾ cup butter or margarine
½ cup chopped onion
1 cup chopped celery
1 cup chicken broth
1 can chicken-and-rice soup

1 (10¾-ounce) can cream of
    chicken soup
2 packages cornbread stuffing
    mix, prepared
1 large broiler-fryer, seasoned,
    cooked, and deboned

Melt butter in a skillet over medium heat. Add onion and celery; sauté until tender. Set aside. Cook broth and soups in a saucepan until thoroughly heated. Pour over cornbread stuffing in a large bowl, stirring well. Add onion mixture. Alternate layers of stuffing mixture and chicken in a greased 13- x 9-inch baking dish, beginning and ending with stuffing mixture. Bake at 350° for 45 minutes.

It Ain't Chili and It Ain't Beans

1 (8-ounce) can pork and beans
4 (16-ounce) cans dark red
    kidney beans
2 packages chili seasoning mix
4 ounces jalapeño relish
1½ ounces cayenne pepper
    or to taste
1½ ounces ground black pepper
    or to taste
1 tablespoon salt

1 ounce liquid smoke
2 pounds ground beef
2 pounds beef sausage
1 pound sharp Cheddar cheese,
    cubed
1 pound mozzarella or
    Monterey Jack cheese, cubed
2 large yellow onions, chopped
1 celery stalk, chopped
2 green bell peppers, chopped

Combine beans in a 3-gallon pot. Place over low heat. Add chili seasoning, liquid smoke, salt, cayenne and black pepper, and jalapeño relish. Stir well. Add cheeses. Microwave sausage on HIGH 4 minutes; cut into bite-size pieces, and fry in a skillet until done. Drain and add sausage to bean mixture. Brown ground beef in skillet; drain and add to bean mixture. Add onion, celery, and bell pepper to mixture. Cover pot, and bring just to a boil. Cook, stirring often, 15 minutes.

Mixture will get spicier as it cooks.

Quick Lasagna

1	pound ground beef		Garlic salt
1	jar spaghetti sauce		Onion powder
3	eggs		Dried Italian seasoning
1	large container cottage cheese		Salt and pepper
2	cups (8-ounces) mozzarella cheese		Dried parsley flakes
½	cup grated Parmesan cheese	16	ounces lasagna noodles, cooked
2	cups (8-ounces) mild Cheddar cheese		

Brown beef in a skillet over medium heat. Drain. Add spaghetti sauce, and simmer, stirring occasionally, 10 minutes. Combine eggs, cheeses, and seasonings. In a 13- x 9-inch baking dish, layer noodles, meat sauce, and cheese, ending with meat sauce. Sprinkle with mozzarella and Cheddar cheeses and dried parsley flakes.

Quiche Lorraine

4	bacon slices, cooked and crumbled	8	thin Swiss cheese slices
4	thin onion slices, sautéed	3	eggs
1	(8-inch) piecrust, baked 10 minutes at 450°	¼	teaspoon dry mustard
8	very thin ham slices	1	cup heated light cream
			Ground nutmeg

Sprinkle half of bacon and onion over bottom of crust. Add half of ham and cheese. Repeat layers. Combine eggs, mustard, and cream. Pour over layers. Let stand 10 minutes. Sprinkle with nutmeg. Bake at 350° for 40 minutes.

Shipwreck

1	large can stewed tomatoes, undrained	1	green bell pepper, finely chopped
1	(16-ounce) can kidney beans, partially drained	6	medium potatoes, peeled and thinly sliced
1	onion, finely chopped	1½	pounds ground beef, browned

Combine tomatoes, beans, onion, and bell pepper. Layer half of potato in a baking dish. Top with half of beef, and half of tomato mixture. Repeat layers. Bake at 350° for 1½ hours, removing lid to boil off liquid, if necessary.

Zoe's Stuffed-Pepper Casserole

6   large green bell peppers, halved and seeded
1¼ pounds lean ground beef
    Olive oil
    Dash of seasoned salt
    Dash of garlic salt
2   teaspoons dried oregano
1   teaspoon dried thyme
1   teaspoon pepper
1   teaspoon dried basil
4   garlic cloves, pressed
1   cup long-grain white rice, cooked
1   onion, finely chopped
1   small green, red, or yellow bell pepper, chopped
1   can Mexican-style stewed tomatoes
    Shredded cheese

Bring bell pepper halves and water to cover to a boil in a large saucepan. Boil until tender; remove to a plate. Cook ground beef in olive oil in a large skillet over medium heat. Add salts, pepper, oregano, thyme, and basil to skillet with beef. As beef begins to brown, add garlic. Stir in three-fourths of onion and chopped bell pepper. Remove from heat. Add remaining onion, chopped bell pepper, and rice. Place over low heat, and add 1 tablespoon olive oil. Add tomatoes, and simmer 5 minutes. Cut a slice from bottoms of bell pepper halves to form a flat base. Arrange pepper halves snugly in a baking dish. Spoon beef mixture over pepper halves. Top with shredded cheese. Bake at 350° for 15 to 20 minutes.

Cajun Gumbo

½   cup all-purpose flour
½   cup vegetable oil
1   large onion, finely chopped
1   large green bell pepper, finely chopped
1   cup finely chopped celery
    Pressed garlic to taste
1   bunch green onions, sliced
    Salt and ground black pepper to taste
    Cayenne pepper
    Cajun seasoning blend (optional)
1   (5- to 7-pound) hen, cut up
1½ cups water
3   pounds smoked sausage, cooked

Place flour and oil in a 12-quart aluminum or stainless steel stockpot. Cook mixture over medium heat, stirring constantly, 20 to 30 minutes or until dark golden brown, being careful not to burn. Add onion, and cook until transparent. Add bell pepper and celery. Reduce heat, and simmer about 15 minutes, adding garlic, green onions, and seasonings to taste. Rub chicken pieces with salt and pepper and desired seasonings, and add to pot with 1½ cups water. Gradually add enough water to cover chicken pieces. Bring gumbo to a low boil. Reduce heat, and simmer 1 hour. Add water to thin, if desired. Cut sausage into 1½-inch pieces. Add to gumbo 15 minutes before serving. Serve with rice.

Cornell Chicken

½	cup vegetable oil	1	egg
1	cup cider vinegar		Skinned and boned chicken
2	tablespoons salt		breast halves
1½	teaspoons poultry seasoning		Buns
½	teaspoon pepper		

Whisk together first 6 ingredients. Place in a shallow dish. Flatten chicken breast halves to ½-inch thickness using a meat mallet. Add chicken to oil mixture, and chill 2 hours or overnight. Drain chicken, discarding marinade. Grill over medium-high heat until done. Serve on buns with desired condiments.

Creamy Chicken-Broccoli Skillet

½ cup mayonnaise
1 pound skinned and boned chicken breast halves, cubed
2 cups water

1 (10-ounce) package frozen chopped broccoli, thawed and drained (or 2 cups fresh broccoli flowerets)
1 (8-ounce) loaf process cheese spread, cubed
2 cups uncooked quick-cooking rice

Cook mayonnaise in a large skillet over medium heat until hot; add chicken, and cook, stirring often, 8 minutes or until done. Add water, broccoli, and cheese. Bring to a boil. Stir in rice. Cover and remove from heat. Let stand 5 minutes.

Chicken-Rice Casserole

½ cup long-grain white rice
Diced celery
Diced onion
1 (10¾-ounce) can cream of chicken soup

½ cup chicken broth
1 broiler-fryer, cut up
All-purpose flour
Melted butter or margarine
Paprika

Combine first 5 ingredients in a greased 13- x 9-inch baking dish. Sprinkle chicken evenly with flour, and place over rice. Sprinkle with butter and paprika. Bake at 325° for 2 hours.

Five-Hour Oven Stew

1½	pounds cubed stew meat	1	large onion
5	medium potatoes	2	beef bouillon cubes
5	carrots	2	cups spicy vegetable juice
5	celery stalks	3	tablespoons tapioca

Combine all ingredients in a Dutch oven. Bake at 275° for 5 hours.

Sloppy Joes

2	pounds ground beef	¼	cup sugar
	Minced onion to taste	2	teaspoons dry mustard
1	can tomato sauce		Salt to taste
½	cup ketchup		Buns
¼	cup vinegar		

Brown ground beef and onion in a skillet over medium heat. Drain. Add remaining ingredients to beef, and simmer 45 minutes. Serve on buns.

Tuna Casserole

1	(10¾-ounce) can cream of mushroom soup	1	(6-ounce) can tuna, drained
		1	cup unsalted peas
½	cup milk	¼	cup crushed potato chips

Combine soup and milk in a baking dish. Add tuna and peas, and sprinkle with potato chips. Bake at 350° for 20 minutes.

Easy Swiss Steak

1	(1½- to 2-inch-thick) round steak	½	teaspoon salt
2	garlic cloves, pressed (optional)	1	(1-ounce) envelope dry onion soup mix
¼	teaspoon pepper	1	(6-ounce) can tomato paste
		⅓	cup dry white wine

Sprinkle just enough soup mix to cover a large, double-layer square of heavy-duty aluminum foil. Season meat with salt and pepper, and place over soup mix. Sprinkle remaining soup mix over meat. Combine tomato paste and wine, and spread over meat. Fold foil snugly over meat. Place directly on oven rack. Bake at 350° for 2½ hours or until tender. Serve with rice.

Swiss Steak

1½ pounds round steak
    All-purpose flour
    Salt and pepper to taste

¼ cup steak sauce
¾ cup ketchup
2-4 cups water

Cut steak into serving pieces, and score tops. Rub with flour, salt, and pepper. Brown steak in a skillet over medium heat. Combine steak sauce, ketchup, and water in a Dutch oven. Add meat, cover, and cook over medium-low heat 2 to 3 hours or until steak is tender.

Ham 'n Cheese Pie

1 cup diced cooked ham
¾ cup (3-ounces) shredded
    Swiss cheese
5 bacon slices, cooked and
    crumbled
¾ cup (3-ounces) shredded
    Cheddar cheese

3 tablespoons chopped onion
3 tablespoons chopped green
    bell pepper
1 cup milk
¼ cup biscuit mix
2 eggs
    Salt and pepper to taste

Combine first 6 ingredients in a 10-inch pie plate. Process milk and next 3 ingredients in a blender 30 to 45 seconds or until smooth. Pour into pie plate. Bake, uncovered, at 350° for 30 to 35 minutes or until lightly browned. Let stand 5 minutes before cutting.

Pork Chops and Spanish Rice

5 (½-inch-thick) pork chops
2 tablespoons vegetable oil
1½ teaspoons salt
¾ teaspoon chili powder
    Dash of pepper
¾ cup long-grain rice
½ cup chopped onion

¼ cup chopped green bell
    pepper
1 (1-pound, 12-ounce) can
    tomatoes
4 green bell pepper rings
    Shredded cheese

Brown chops in hot oil in a skillet over medium heat. Sprinkle with salt, chili powder, and pepper. Add rice, onion, and bell pepper. Pour tomatoes over top. Cover and simmer, stirring occasionally, 30 to 35 minutes. Add bell pepper rings, and cook 5 more minutes or until rice and chops are tender. Sprinkle with cheese.

Precooked rice may be used; add during last 5 minutes of cooking.

Egg Casserole

1	pound ground sausage	1½	cups (6-ounces) shredded
6	eggs		Cheddar cheese
2	cups milk	1	(4-ounce) can mushroom
1	teaspoon salt		pieces
1	teaspoon dry mustard		Minced onion (optional)
6	bread slices, cubed		

Brown sausage in a skillet over medium heat. Drain and set aside. Beat eggs and milk in a large bowl. Add remaining ingredients, stirring well. Pour into a greased 13- x 9-inch baking dish; chill 8 hours. Bake at 350° for 40 minutes.

Breakfast Pizza

1	pound ground sausage or cooked bacon slices	3	eggs
2	cups biscuit mix	2	tablespoons milk
½	cup cold water	½	teaspoon salt
1	cup frozen hash browns, thawed	⅛	teaspoon pepper
1	cup (4-ounces) shredded Cheddar cheese	2	teaspoons grated Parmesan cheese

Brown sausage in a skillet over medium heat. Drain. Combine biscuit mix and water to form a soft dough. Press dough onto bottom and up sides of an ungreased 13- x 9-inch baking dish. Spoon sausage over dough, and sprinkle with hash browns and Cheddar cheese. Beat eggs, milk, salt, and pepper together. Pour egg mixture over Cheddar cheese. Sprinkle with Parmesan cheese. Bake at 400° for 20 to 25 minutes or until eggs are set.

Chicken-Pasta Toss

16	ounces bow tie pasta	1	cup dried tomatoes packed in oil, cut into strips
1	cup broccoli flowerets	4	teaspoons olive oil, drained from tomatoes
2	skinned and boned chicken breast halves, cooked and cut into strips	1	cup grated Parmesan cheese

Cook pasta in a large saucepan in boiling water just until tender. Do not drain. Add broccoli to pasta in saucepan; cook 3 minutes. Drain pasta and broccoli. Toss all ingredients together in a serving bowl.

Breakfast Sausage Casserole

1	pound ground sausage	8	eggs, well beaten
1	large onion, chopped	4	cups milk
12	bread slices, quartered	1½	teaspoons salt
1	(10-ounce) package sharp Cheddar cheese, shredded	¼	teaspoon pepper
		½	teaspoon dry mustard

Brown sausage in a skillet over medium heat. Drain and remove sausage, reserving 2 tablespoons drippings in skillet. Sauté onion in reserved drippings until transparent. In a 13- x 9-inch baking dish, layer one-half each of bread, sausage, onion, and cheese. Repeat layers once. Beat eggs and next 4 ingredients together; pour over casserole. Cover and chill 8 hours. Let stand at room temperature 1 hour before baking. Bake, uncovered, at 350° for 50 minutes.

Pete's Southwestern Pasta

1	package fajita marinade mix	1	cup skim milk
¼	cup water	½	cup (2-ounces) Monterey Jack cheese with peppers
2	skinned and boned chicken breast halves	1	(15½-ounce) can black beans, drained and rinsed
2	tablespoons butter or margarine	1	(11-ounce) jar salsa
2	tablespoons all-purpose flour	16	ounces penne pasta, cooked
¼	teaspoon salt	1	tomato, diced
⅛	teaspoon cracked black peppercorns	2	green onions, sliced

Whisk together water and fajita marinade. Pour over chicken; cover and chill 2 hours. Drain chicken, discarding marinade. Grill chicken over medium heat until done; cut into strips. Melt butter in a saucepan over low heat. Stir in flour, salt, and pepper. Cook, stirring constantly, until mixture is smooth and bubbly. Stir in milk, and bring to a boil, stirring constantly. Add cheese, stirring until melted. Keep sauce mixture warm. Combine beans and salsa in a saucepan; cook over medium-low heat until hot. Place pasta on warm serving plates. Spoon bean mixture over pasta; top with tomato, onions, and chicken. Drizzle with sauce mixture.

Cream Cheese Spaghetti

1 package spaghetti
2 tablespoons chopped fresh parsley
2 tablespoons freshly ground basil
¼ cup melted butter or margarine
3 garlic cloves, diced
1 (8-ounce) package cream cheese, cubed
¼ cup olive oil
½ cup grated Parmesan cheese

Cook spaghetti according to package directions. Do not drain. Sauté parsley and basil in butter in a large skillet over medium heat. Add garlic, and cook 5 minutes. Add cream cheese, and cook over medium heat, stirring slowly, until blended. Gradually pour in olive oil; stir in Parmesan cheese. Add ½ cup hot water from spaghetti pot, and stir until mixture is consistency of cream sauce. Drain spaghetti, and add to sauce mixture; serve hot.

Enchilada Pie

2 pounds ground beef
2 (16-ounce) can chili beans
2 (16-ounce) can potatoes, sliced
1 (10¾-ounce) can cream of celery soup
1 (12-ounce) jar enchilada sauce
1 small onion, diced
1 package flour tortilla shells
1 (12-ounce) package shredded Cheddar cheese
   Shredded lettuce, diced tomato, sour cream

Brown beef in a skillet over medium heat. Drain. Add chili beans and potato to beef, stirring well. Simmer until thoroughly heated. Combine soup and enchilada sauce in a small bowl; set aside. Spread onion in bottom of a 13- x 9-inch baking dish. Top with ½ each of tortilla shells, soup mixture, and beef mixture. Repeat layers, and sprinkle with cheese. Bake at 350° for 45 minutes. Serve with desired toppings.

Sauce for Meat Loaf

⅓ cup packed brown sugar
¼ cup ketchup
2 teaspoons dry mustard
¼ teaspoon ground nutmeg

Combine all ingredients, and pour over meat loaf just before serving.

Chicken Supreme

8	skinned and boned chicken breast halves	1	(10¾-ounce) can reduced-fat cream of chicken soup
1	can French fried onions, crushed	1	(10¾-ounce) can reduced-fat cream of celery soup
1	cup (4-ounces) finely shredded Cheddar cheese	¼	cup white wine

Place chicken in a 14- x 11-inch baking dish. Cover with crushed onions; top with cheese. Whisk together soups and wine; spoon over chicken. Bake, covered with aluminum foil, at 350° for 30 minutes. Uncover and bake 30 more minutes. Serve with rice and glazed carrots.

Slow Cooker Pizza

1½	pounds ground beef	12	ounces wide egg noodles, cooked
1	onion or green bell pepper, chopped	1	package pepperoni slices
1	(8-ounce) can pizza sauce	1	(8-ounce) package shredded reduced fat Cheddar cheese, divided
1	(16-ounce) can spaghetti sauce		
1	(4-ounce) can sliced mushrooms	1	(8-ounce) package shredded reduced fat mozzarella cheese, divided

Brown ground beef in a skillet over medium heat. Drain; stir in onion, and set aside. Combine pizza sauce, spaghetti sauce, and mushrooms in a bowl. Layer noodles, beef mixture, sauce mixture, pepperoni, and half each of cheeses in a 5-quart slow cooker. Cook on HIGH 2 to 4 hours. Stir in remaining half of cheeses just before serving.

Flank Steak Marinade

½	cup soy sauce	1½	teaspoons garlic powder
2	tablespoons vinegar	1½	teaspoons ground ginger
3	tablespoons honey	3 to 4	green onion stalks, chopped
¾	cup vegetable oil		

Combine all ingredients in a large shallow dish. Score flank steak on both sides, and add to marinade. Chill at least 8 hours, turning once.

Pizza-Style Spaghetti

16	ounces thin spaghetti	½	teaspoon dried Italian
2	eggs		seasoning
1	cup milk	1	(4-ounce) can sliced
1	(32-ounce) jar spaghetti sauce		mushrooms
1	pound ground beef	1	package pepperoni slices
1	medium onion, chopped	2	cups (8-ounces) shredded
¼	teaspoon minced garlic		mozzarella cheese

Break spaghetti into bite-size pieces, and cook according to package directions. Drain and place in a large bowl. Beat eggs and milk; add to spaghetti. Pour mixture into a 13- x 9-inch baking dish. Top with spaghetti sauce. Brown ground beef and onion in a skillet over medium heat. Drain. Stir in Parmesan cheese. Stir garlic and Italian seasoning into beef mixture. Spread beef mixture over sauce. Sprinkle with mushrooms. Arrange pepperoni over mushrooms, and top with mozzarella cheese. Bake at 350° for 40 minutes. Let stand 5 minutes before cutting.

MaryElla's Smooth-and-Spicy Spaghetti Sauce

1	(15-ounce) can tomato sauce	⅛	teaspoon crushed red pepper
2	(12-ounce) cans tomato juice	⅛	teaspoon cayenne pepper
1	(6-ounce) can tomato paste	½	teaspoon chili powder
¾	cup water	¼	teaspoon dried oregano
1	tablespoon honey	½	teaspoon dried basil
¼	teaspoon cracked black peppercorns	1	tablespoon dried parsley flakes
1	teaspoon Worcestershire sauce	1	garlic clove, pressed
		2	green onions, sliced
1	bay leaf		

Combine tomato sauce, juice, and paste in a large cast-iron skillet. Add remaining ingredients, and bring just to a boil over medium-high heat. Reduce heat, and simmer 1 hour. Serve over pasta.

Ham Glaze

1	cup honey	1	cup packed brown sugar
½	cup wine vinegar	½	cup prepared mustard

Combine all ingredients, stirring well. Spoon over ham before baking, and use to baste during baking.

Brandied Tomato Gravy

1	(8-ounce) can tomatoes	1	(14½-ounce) can beef broth
4	tablespoons butter or margarine	1	tablespoon brandy
		½	teaspoon meat extract paste
2	tablespoons all-purpose flour	¼	teaspoon salt

Drain tomatoes, reserving liquid. Finely chop tomatoes, and set aside. Melt butter in a 1-quart saucepan over medium heat; stir in flour, and cook, stirring occasionally, 1 minute. Gradually stir in broth, reserved tomato liquid, chopped tomato, brandy, meat extract paste, and salt. Cook, stirring constantly, until gravy thickens and boils.

Meat extract paste, a concentrated extract of meat with seasonings, is available at supermarkets.

Giblet Gravy

	Turkey heart, gizzard, liver, and neck meat	3	tablespoons all-purpose flour
1	celery stalk, chopped	2	cups giblet broth
1	onion, chopped		Salt and pepper to taste
4	tablespoons roasted turkey drippings	2	hard-cooked eggs, chopped

Cook turkey parts in boiling water to cover until tender. Drain and cool before chopping. Combine drippings and flour in a saucepan over medium heat; add broth, and cook, stirring constantly, until gravy thickens. Add salt and pepper; stir in chopped meat and egg. Cook until thoroughly heated.

Sausage Gravy

1	pound ground sausage	¼	teaspoon ground nutmeg
2	tablespoons minced onion	¼	teaspoon poultry seasoning
6	tablespoons all-purpose flour		Dash of Worcestershire sauce
1	quart milk		Dash of hot sauce

Brown sausage in a large skillet over medium heat (do not allow it to get crisp), adding onion just as sausage begins to brown. Drain, reserving 2 tablespoons drippings. Stir in flour; cook, stirring often, 6 to 7 minutes. Pour in milk, and add remaining ingredients. Cook until thoroughly heated. Serve over biscuits.

Apricot Glaze

1 (17-ounce) can apricot halves, drained
2 tablespoons sugar
2 tablespoons vegetable oil
2 tablespoons white vinegar
1 teaspoon salt
¼ teaspoon ground cloves

Process all ingredients at medium speed in a blender until smooth.

Apple-Mustard Glaze

1 (11-ounce) jar apple jelly
⅓ cup dry white wine
3 tablespoons minced green onions
3 tablespoons prepared mustard
1½ teaspoons salt
¾ teaspoon curry powder
½ teaspoon cracked black peppercorns

Cook all ingredients in a 1-quart saucepan over medium heat, stirring often, 5 minutes or until jelly melts.

Honey-and-Spice Glaze

2 medium lemons
½ cup honey
2 tablespoons mixed pickling spice, crushed
2 teaspoons salt

Cut rind from lemons, and remove white membrane. Cut rind lengthwise into thin strips. Squeeze 3 tablespoons juice from lemon sections. Cook lemon rind, juice, and remaining ingredients in a 1-quart saucepan over medium heat about 5 minutes.

Never-Fail Dumplings

1 egg
¼ cup milk
1 cup all-purpose flour
¼ teaspoon salt
2 teaspoons baking powder
Chicken broth

Beat egg and milk together. Add next 3 ingredients, stirring until blended. Bring broth to a boil in a large saucepan. Drop dumplings into broth; cover and boil 15 minutes.

Breads

Keith Harlin
Kidney transplant recipient,
2007

Keith received his kidney transplant in June 2007. He loves fishing and other water activities.

Pear Bread

2-3 fresh pears or 1 (16-ounce)
    can pears, drained
½ cup vegetable oil
1 cup sugar
2 eggs
¼ cup sour cream
1 teaspoon vanilla extract

2 cups all-purpose flour
½ teaspoon salt
1 teaspoon baking soda
¼ teaspoon ground cinnamon
¼ teaspoon ground nutmeg
½ cup chopped nuts

Cut pears in half, and mash to equal 1 cup. Beat oil and sugar at medium speed with an electric mixer until blended; add eggs, 1 at a time, beating after each. Add sour cream and vanilla; set aside. Sift together flour and next 4 ingredients. Add to oil mixture. Beat well. Add pears and nuts to oil mixture. Pour into loaf pans, and bake at 350° for 45 minutes.

Irish Soda Bread

4 cups buttermilk
2 eggs
¼ teaspoon baking soda
7 cups all-purpose flour

2 cups raisins
½ cup sugar
5 teaspoons baking powder
2 teaspoons salt

Beat first 3 ingredients at medium speed with an electric mixer until blended. Set aside. Combine remaining ingredients in a large bowl. Stir in buttermilk mixture, blending well. Pour into 3 large greased and floured loaf pans. Bake at 375° for 45 minutes to 1 hour.

Christmas Bread

1 (8-ounce) package cream
    cheese, softened
1 cup butter or margarine
1½ cups sugar
1½ teaspoons vanilla extract
4 eggs

2¼ cups cake flour
1½ teaspoons baking powder
1 (10-ounce) jar maraschino
    cherries, finely chopped
½ cup chopped nuts

Beat first 4 ingredients at medium speed with an electric mixer. Add eggs 1 at a time, beating well after each addition. Gradually add 2 cups flour and baking powder. Combine ¼ cup flour, cherries, and nuts; fold into cream cheese mixture. Bake in 4 small greased and floured loaf pans at 325° for 1 hour.

Poppy Seed Bread

3 cups all-purpose flour
1½ teaspoons salt
1½ teaspoons baking powder
3 eggs, beaten
1½ cups milk
1½ cups vegetable oil

2¼ cups sugar
1½ tablespoons poppy seeds
1½ teaspoons vanilla extract
1½ teaspoons butter flavoring
1½ teaspoons almond flavoring
Glaze

Beat first 11 ingredients at medium speed with an electric mixer. Pour into 2 greased and floured 9- x 5-inch loaf pans. Bake at 350° for 1 hour. Cool in pans 5 minutes. Pour glaze over top. Cool 10 minutes. Remove from pans.

Glaze

¼ cup orange juice
¾ cup sugar
½ teaspoon almond flavoring

½ teaspoon butter flavoring
½ teaspoon vanilla extract

Cook all ingredients in a saucepan just until sugar dissolves.

Buttermilk Bread

5¾-6¼ cups all-purpose flour
3 tablespoons sugar
2½ teaspoons salt
¼ teaspoon baking soda

1 (¼-ounce) envelope active dry yeast
1 cup buttermilk
1 cup water
⅓ cup butter or margarine

Combine 2 cups flour and next 4 ingredients in a large mixing bowl; set aside. Cook buttermilk, water, and butter in a saucepan over low heat until mixture is warm (120° to 130°). (Butter doesn't need to melt.) Gradually add buttermilk mixture to dry ingredients. Beat at medium speed with an electric mixer 2 minutes. Add ¾ cup flour. Beat at high speed 2 minutes. Stir in enough remaining flour to make a stiff dough. Turn out onto a floured surface, and knead until smooth and elastic. Place in a greased bowl; turn to grease top. Cover and let rise 1 hour. Punch dough down, and divide in half. Place in 2 greased loaf pans. Cover and let rise about 1 hour. Bake at 375° for 30 to 35 minutes. Remove from pans to cool.

Greek Bread

2 small packages grated
 mozzarella cheese
 Minced garlic to taste
 Chopped green onions to
 taste

½ cup chopped ripe olives
1 cup mayonnaise
½ cup butter or margarine,
 softened
 French bread

Combine mayonnaise and butter, beating until soft. Add remaining ingredients, and spread on French bread. Bake at 350° for 20 minutes.

Cranberry Nut Bread

2 cups fresh or canned
 cranberries, halved
¾ cup chopped nuts
2 tablespoons butter or
 margarine, melted
2 cups flour
1 cup plus 2 tablespoons sugar

1¾ teaspoons baking powder
1 teaspoon salt
½ teaspoon baking soda
1 egg, beaten
⅓ cup orange juice
¼ cup water

Grease bottom only of a loaf pan, and line with greased wax paper. Rinse and sort cranberries. Sift together flour, sugar, baking powder, salt, and soda. Set aside. Combine egg, orange juice, and water; stir in butter. Make a well in center of dry ingredients; add liquids. Stir only until moistened; add berries and nuts, and stir until blended. Turn into pan. Bake at 350° 70 minutes. Cool in pan on a rack 10 minutes. Remove from pan, and peel off wax paper. Turn right side up, and cool. Store in aluminum foil.

Finnish Pancakes

5 eggs
¾ cup sugar
¼ teaspoon salt

1½ cups milk
1 cup flour
¼ cup butter or margarine

Beat together eggs, sugar, and salt. Add milk and flour, and mix well. Melt butter in a 400° oven in a heavy skillet. Dump mixture into hot butter. Bake at 400° for 25 minutes. Serve warm with syrup, honey, or jam.

Banana Nut Bread

1½	cups sifted all-purpose flour	¾	cup vegetable oil
¾	teaspoon baking soda	3	tablespoons buttermilk
¼	teaspoon salt	1	cup mashed banana (about
1	cup sugar		2 large)
2	eggs, lightly beaten	½	cup chopped pecans

Grease and flour a loaf pan. Stir together flour, soda, and salt in a mixing bowl. Add sugar, eggs, oil, and buttermilk. Stir to blend. Stir in banana and pecans. Pour batter into prepared pan. Bake at 325° for 1 hour and 10 minutes. Cool in pan on wire rack 15 minutes. Remove from pan, and cool completely on rack.

For an extra-moist bread, wrap warm loaf tightly after removing from pan.

Easy French Bread

5	cups all-purpose flour	2	(¼-ounce) envelopes active
1	tablespoon olive oil		dry yeast
1½	teaspoons salt	2	cups warm water

Combine first 4 ingredients in a food processor. Add warm water, and process 2 to 3 minutes. Turn out onto a floured surface, and shape into a ball. Place in a greased bowl, turning to grease top. Let rise 1 hour or until doubled in bulk. Punch dough down, and divide into 3 portions. Shape portions into long logs, and place in oiled baguette pans. Let rise 15 minutes. Bake at 425° for 25 minutes.

French Bread

5	cups all-purpose flour	2	(¼-ounce) envelopes active
1	tablespoon olive oil		dry yeast
1½	teaspoons salt	2	cups warm water

Combine 3 cups flour and remaining ingredients in a bowl, and mix using hand mixer. Turn dough out onto a floured surface. Add about 2 cups flour, mixing with hands after each addition until dough forms a ball that can be kneaded. Knead 5 to 8 minutes. Place in a greased bowl; turn to grease top. Let rise 1 hour or until doubled in bulk. Punch dough down, and divide into 3 portions. Shape portions into long logs, and place in oiled baguette pans. Let rise 15 minutes. Bake at 425° for 25 minutes.

Overnight Coffee Cake

2	cups all-purpose flour	2	eggs, beaten
½	teaspoon salt	1	cup buttermilk
1	teaspoon ground cinnamon	½	cup packed brown sugar
1	teaspoon baking powder	¼	cup sugar
1	teaspoon baking soda	2	tablespoons all-purpose flour
1	cup sugar	¼	cup butter or margarine,
½	cup packed brown sugar		melted
⅔	cup butter or margarine, creamed	1½	cups chopped pecans

Sift together first 5 ingredients; add sugar and next 4 ingredients. Pour into a greased 13-x 9-inch pan. Combine ½ cup brown sugar and remaining ingredients. Spread over batter. Cover and chill at least 8 hours. Bake at 350° for 35 minutes.

Cranberry Coffee Cake

½	cup butter or margarine	1	cup sour cream
1	cup sugar	1	(8-ounce) can whole-berry
2	eggs		cranberry sauce
1	teaspoon almond extract	1	tablespoon butter or
2	cups flour		margarine, melted
¾	teaspoon baking soda	1	cup powdered sugar
1	teaspoon baking powder	1-2	tablespoons warm water
½	teaspoon salt	½	teaspoon almond extract

Beat ½ cup butter and sugar at medium speed with an electric mixer until creamy. Beat in eggs and extract. Combine flour and next 3 ingredients; stir into butter mixture alternately with sour cream. Spread half of mixture into a greased and floured 10-inch tube pan. Spread cranberry sauce over batter, and top with remaining batter. Bake at 350° for 55 to 60 minutes. Cool in pan 10 minutes. Remove from pan to cool completely. Combine melted butter and next 3 ingredients. Drizzle over cooled cake.

Beer Bread

3	cups self-rising flour	1	(12-ounce) can beer
3	tablespoons sugar	½	cup melted butter

Combine first three ingredients, mixing quickly. Pour into a loaf pan. Bake at 350° for 45 minutes. Pour ½ cup melted butter over top, and bake 10 to 15 more minutes.

Mexican Cornbread

2 cups self-rising corn meal
1 egg, lightly beaten
1 (8-ounce) can cream-style corn
⅓ cup diced jalapeño

1 cup (4 ounces) shredded Cheddar cheese
2 tablespoons vegetable oil
Milk

Combine first 6 ingredients with enough milk to make a batter. Pour into a preheated, greased cast-iron skillet. Bake at 350° for 20 to 30 minutes.

Cheese Biscuits

2 cups self-rising flour
3 heaping tablespoons shortening

½ cup (2 ounces) shredded Cheddar cheese
¾ cup milk

Cut flour and shortening together with a pastry blender until blended. Add cheese and milk. Turn dough out onto floured wax paper; sprinkle flour over dough. Pat dough out, and cut with biscuit cutter. Place on foil-covered baking sheets. (You may cover with foil and freeze at this point). Bake at 450° for 12 to 15 minutes.

Biscuits

2 cups self-rising flour
¼ cup shortening

¾ cup buttermilk

Cut shortening and flour together with a pastry blender until blended. Add buttermilk. Stir with a fork. Turn out onto floured wax paper; knead until smooth. Roll out to ½-inch thickness. Cut with biscuit cutter. Bake at 450° for 10 to 12 minutes.

Fresh Apple Muffins

1½ cups all-purpose flour
1 cup sugar
1 teaspoon baking soda
1 teaspoon ground cinnamon
1 teaspoon salt

2 eggs
¾ cup vegetable oil
2 Granny Smith apples, diced
1 cup chopped pecans
1 cup raisins (optional)

Combine all ingredients; pour into paper-lined muffin pans. Bake at 350° for 25 to 30 minutes.

Caramel Pull-Aparts

3   (10- to 12-ounce) cans   ½   cup packed brown sugar
     refrigerated biscuits   ½   cup butter or margarine
     Cinnamon-sugar   ½   cup vanilla ice cream
½   cup sugar

Cut each biscuit into fourths, and roll in cinnamon-sugar. Arrange in a greased 13- x 9-inch pan. Cook remaining ingredients in a saucepan over low heat until melted. Spread over tops of biscuits. Bake 350° for 15 to 20 minutes. Invert onto foil-lined baking sheet.

Sour Cream Coffee Cake

½   cup butter or margarine   1¾   cups all-purpose flour
1   cup sugar   ¼   teaspoon salt
2   eggs   ⅓   cup packed brown sugar
1   teaspoon vanilla extract   ¼   cup sugar
1   cup sour cream   ½   cup chopped nuts
1   teaspoon baking soda   2   teaspoons ground cinnamon
1   teaspoon baking powder   1   can fruit pie filling (any flavor)

Beat first 9 ingredients until smooth. Pour half of batter into a greased 13- x 9-inch pan. Combine ⅓ cup brown sugar and next 3 ingredients. Sprinkle half of mixture over batter layer. Spread with pie filling. Top with remaining batter and then rest of topping. Bake at 325° for 40 to 45 minutes.

Zucchini Nut Muffins

1½ cups self-rising flour   ½   cup vegetable oil
1   teaspoon ground cinnamon   1   cup sugar
½   teaspoon ground nutmeg   ½   cup chopped pecans
1   cup grated zucchini   2-4 tablespoons water
1   egg

Combine first 3 ingredients. Set aside. Combine zucchini, egg, and oil; add to dry ingredients, stirring just until moistened. Add pecans and water. Spoon into lightly greased muffin pans. Bake at 350° for 30 minutes.

Carrot Muffins

1½	cups self-rising flour	2	large carrots, grated
½	cup packed brown sugar	⅓	cup vegetable oil
2	eggs	1	teaspoon ground cinnamon

Combine flour and sugar. Set aside. Combine eggs, carrot, and oil; add to dry ingredients, stirring just until moistened. Bake at 350° for 30 minutes.

Apple-Cream Coffee Cake

½	cup butter or margarine	1	teaspoon baking soda
1	cup sugar	1	cup sour cream
2	eggs	1	apple, peeled, cored, and
1	teaspoon vanilla extract		thinly sliced
2	cups all-purpose flour	½	cup chopped walnuts
1	teaspoon baking powder	2	teaspoons ground cinnamon
½	teaspoon salt	½	cup sugar

Grease a 9-inch angel food pan with removable bottom. Beat butter until creamy; add sugar, and beat until fluffy. Add eggs, 1 at a time, and blend in vanilla. Add dry ingredients alternately with sour cream. Spread half of batter into pan. Top with apple. Combine walnuts, cinnamon, and sugar. Sprinkle half of mixture over batter. Repeat batter and nut mixture layers. Bake at 375° for 40 minutes. Let stand in pan on a wire rack 30 minutes. Loosen edges, and remove from pan. When completely cool, remove from base of pan.

Batter will be very stiff.

Apple Bread

¾	cup sugar	1	teaspoon baking soda
½	cup shortening	½	teaspoon salt
2	eggs	2	cups chopped apple
1	teaspoon vanilla extract	½	cup chopped nuts
2	cups all-purpose flour	1	tablespoon sugar
¾	teaspoon baking powder	¼	teaspoon ground cinnamon

Beat sugar, shortening, eggs, and vanilla at medium speed with an electric mixer until blended. Stir in dry ingredients until smooth. Add apple and nuts, and spread into a greased and floured 9- x 5-inch loaf pan. Sprinkle with sugar and cinnamon. Bake at 375° for 50 to 60 minutes. Remove from pan immediately.

Pumpkin Swirl Bread

1	(8-ounce) package cream cheese, softened	½	teaspoon salt
¼	cup sugar	¼	teaspoon ground nutmeg
1	egg, beaten	1	cup pumpkin
1¾	cups all-purpose flour	½	cup butter or margarine,
1½	cups sugar		melted
1	teaspoon baking soda	1	egg, beaten
1	teaspoon ground cinnamon	⅓	cup water

Combine first 3 ingredients; set aside. Combine flour and next 5 ingredients in a large bowl. Combine pumpkin and next 3 ingredients; add to flour mixture, stirring just until moistened. Reserve 2 cup batter. Pour remaining batter into a greased and floured 9- x 5-inch loaf pan. Pour cream cheese mixture over top. Spread with reserved pumpkin batter. Cut through with a knife for swirl effect. Bake at 350° for 1 hour and 10 minutes. Cool 5 minutes in pan, and remove.

Oven-Baked French Toast

1	loaf French bread, sliced ¾-inch thick	2	tablespoons corn syrup
1	cup packed brown sugar	6	eggs
½	cup butter or margarine	2	cups milk
		1½	teaspoons vanilla extract

Cook brown sugar, butter, and syrup in a saucepan over medium heat until of syrup consistency. Pour into a greased 13- x 9-inch pan. Arrange bread slices over sugar mixture. Beat eggs, milk, and vanilla together until blended. Pour over bread. Bake, uncovered, at 350° for 40 to 45 minutes. Serve with bacon or sausage.

Spicy Zucchini Bread

1	cup vegetable oil	3	teaspoons ground cinnamon
2	cups sugar	1	teaspoon baking soda
3	eggs	½	teaspoon baking powder
2	cups shredded zucchini	1	cup chopped walnuts
3	cups all-purpose flour		

Beat oil and sugar at medium speed with an electric mixer until blended. Beat in eggs, 1 at a time; stir in zucchini. Sift flour, cinnamon, soda, and baking powder; add to oil mixture, beating until blended. Fold in nuts. Pour into a greased and floured 9- x 5-inch loaf pan. Bake at 325° for 1 hour.

Miniature Rolls

1⅓ cups all-purpose
⅓ cup sugar
2 teaspoons baking powder
½ teaspoon salt
½ cup milk

2 eggs, beaten
¼ cup butter or margarine, melted
Melted butter or margarine

Sift together first 4 ingredients. Combine milk and eggs; add to dry ingredients, stirring well. Stir in ¼ cup butter. Spoon batter into well-greased miniature muffin cups, filling two-thirds full. Bake at 400° for 15 minutes or until golden. Brush tops with melted butter.

Cinnamon Butterfly Rolls

½ cup sugar
1 teaspoon salt
1 (¼-ounce) envelope active dry yeast
4⅓ cups all-purpose flour
1 cup milk
2 teaspoons vanilla extract

2 eggs
½ cup packed brown sugar
½ cup chopped pecans
½ cup raisins
1 teaspoon ground cinnamon
Butter or margarine

Combine sugar, salt, yeast, and 1 cup flour. In a 1-quart saucepan over low heat, heat milk and ½ cup butter until very warm (120° to 130°). Butter doesn't need to melt. With electric mixer at low speed, gradually beat milk mixture into dry ingredients just until blended. Increase speed to medium; beat 2 minutes. Add vanilla, 1 egg, and 1 cup flour to form a thick batter; continue beating 2 minutes. With wooden spoon, stir in 2 cups flour to form a soft dough. Turn out onto floured surface; knead until smooth and elastic, about 10 minutes, working in about ⅓ cup more flour. Shape into ball; place in large greased bowl, turning to grease top. Cover, let rise in warm place until doubled in bulk. Punch dough down. Turn out onto lightly flour surface. Cut into 2 portions. Cover and let rest 15 minutes. Combine brown sugar and next 3 ingredients. Melt 4 tablespoons butter in a small saucepan. With floured rolling pin, roll half of dough into a 17- x 12-inch rectangle. Brush with half of melted butter; sprinkle with half of brown sugar mixture. Roll up, jellyroll fashion, starting at long side; pinch seam to seal. Cut roll into 9 wedges, 2½ inches at wide side and 1 inch at short side. Turn wedges short side up. Press handle of wooden spoon across each. Repeat with other dough portion. Place rolls 2 inches apart on greased baking sheets. Cover and let rise in a warm place until doubled. Beat remaining egg; brush over rolls. Bake at 350° for 20 minutes or until golden. Remove to wire racks to cool.

Quick-and-Easy Rolls

1	cup self-rising flour	1	heaping tablespoon
1	tablespoon sugar		mayonnaise
		½	cup sweet milk

Combine all ingredients. Spoon into muffin pans. Bake at 450° until golden.

Refrigerator Roll Dough

2	(¼-ounce) active dry yeast	¼	cup shortening
2	cups warm water (105° to	1	large egg
	115°)	2	teaspoons salt
½	cup sugar	7	cups all-purpose flour

Dissolve yeast in warm water in large mixer bowl. Stir in sugar, shortening, egg, salt, and 3 cups flour. Beat until smooth. Stir in enough remaining flour to make dough easy to handle. Place dough in greased bowl; turn to grease top. Cover loosely with plastic wrap; chill at least 2 hours or until ready to use. (Dough can be kept up to 4 days in refrigerator at 45° or below. Keep covered.) Punch down dough; divide. Shape on lightly floured surface and let rise as directed below. Heat oven to 400°. Bake as directed. Using ¼ of the dough, shape bits into 1 inch balls, tucking edges under so they resemble caps. Place in lightly greased 8 inch round layer pan or pie pan. Cover for about 1 hour. Brush 1 tablespoon melted butter over rolls. Bake until rolls are golden brown, about 15 minutes.

Rolls

2	(¼-ounce) envelopes active	1	cup instant potatoes (made
	dry yeast		up)
4	cups warm water		All-purpose flour
1	cup instant nonfat dry milk		Melted butter or margarine for
1	cup sugar		top of rolls
1	cup butter or margarine		

Dissolve yeast in warm water in large bowl with 1 teaspoon sugar; let stand 5 minutes until bubbly. Add dry ingredients, milk, and sugar to hot potatoes and butter, then mix with yeast mixture in mixer with 4 cups flour. Blend till smooth, then add flour to make soft dough. Place in a large greased bowl. Chill 4 to 24 hours. Shape in rolls of your choice. Let rise until doubled in bulk. Bake at 350° for 12 to 15 minutes.

Best-Ever Piecrust

1 cup shortening
3 cups sifted flour
1 teaspoon salt

1 egg
1 teaspoon vinegar
5 teaspoons water

Cut shortening into flour until crumbly. Beat egg in a cup; add water and vinegar. Add egg mixture to vinegar mixture. Add salt and blend until it holds together. Turn dough out onto a floured surface. Roll to desired size circle. Makes 3 crusts.

Baked Graham Cracker Crumb Crust

For 8-inch crust:
1¼ cups graham cracker crumbs
4 tablespoons butter or margarine, melted
3 tablespoons sugar

For 9-inch crust:
1½ cups graham cracker crumbs
6 tablespoons butter or margarine, melted
¼ cup sugar

Combine all ingredients in a pie plate. Press onto bottom and up sides of plate. Bake at 375° for 8 minutes. Cool on a wire rack.

Blueberry Muffins

¼ cup sugar
1 cup fresh blueberries
1½ cups all-purpose flour
¼ cup sugar
2 teaspoons baking powder

2 eggs or 4 egg whites
½ cup milk
¼ cup melted butter or margarine, slightly cooled

Toss ¼ cup sugar and berries together; set aside. Combine flour, ¼ cup sugar, and baking powder in a large bowl. Beat eggs in a smaller bowl; stir in milk and melted butter. Quickly stir into dry ingredients, stirring just until blended. Gently stir in berries. Spoon into greased muffin pans. Sprinkle tops with sugar, if desired. Bake at 400° for 20 to 25 minutes.

Cakes, Pies, Desserts & Cookies

Kyle Curry
Liver transplant recipient,
2000

Kyle received his liver transplant in December 2000 when he was only 15 months old. Today, he is active and healthy and requires only one medication.

Turtle Cake

1	package German chocolate cake mix	1	can sweetened condensed milk
1	(14-ounce) package caramel candies	1	cup (6 ounces) semisweet chocolate morsels
½	cup butter or margarine	1	cup pecans, chopped

Prepare cake batter according to package directions. Pour about half of batter into a greased and floured 13- x 9-inch pan. Bake at 350° for 15 minutes. Cool in pan. Melt caramels in a saucepan over medium heat. Add butter, stirring until melted. Remove from heat. Add milk, blending well. Pour over cooled cake. Sprinkle morsels, then pecans over caramel mixture. Pour remaining batter over top. Bake at 350° for 30 minutes. Serve with ice cream.

Ugly Duckling Pudding Cake

1	package yellow cake mix	4	eggs
1	package lemon instant pudding mix	¼	cup vegetable oil
		½	cup chopped nuts
1	(16-ounce) can fruit cocktail	½	cup packed brown sugar
1	cup flaked coconut		Butter Glaze

Beat first 6 ingredients at medium speed with an electric mixer 4 minutes. Pour into a greased and floured 13- x 9-inch pan. Sprinkle with brown sugar and nuts. Bake at 325° for 45 minutes or until cake springs back when touched. Cool in pan 15 minutes. Spoon hot Butter Glaze over warm cake.

Butter Glaze

½	cup butter	½	cup evaporated milk
½	cup sugar	1⅓	cups flaked coconut

Bring first 3 ingredients to a boil in a saucepan. Boil 2 minutes. Stir in coconut.

Two-Step Cheesecake

1	cup all-purpose flour	8	tablespoons sugar
½	teaspoon baking powder	1	teaspoon vanilla extract
	Pinch of salt	1	teaspoon lemon juice
4	tablespoons sugar	1	tablespoon all-purpose flour
2	ounces melted butter	4	eggs
1	egg	2	cups (2%) milk
1	(8-ounce) package cream cheese, softened		

Combine first 6 ingredients; press into bottom and up sides of a 9-inch round cake pan. Process remaining ingredients in a blender until smooth. Pour into crust. Bake at 350° for 50 minutes. Chill at least 24 hours before serving. You may sprinkle with ground cinnamon before baking or top with fruit just before serving.

One-Step Pound Cake

2¼	cups all-purpose flour	1	teaspoon vanilla extract
2	cups sugar	3	eggs
½	teaspoon salt	1	teaspoon grated lemon rind
½	teaspoon baking powder	1	cup powdered sugar
1	cup sour cream	1-2	tablespoons lemon juice
1	cup butter or margarine		

Beat first 9 ingredients at low speed with an electric mixer until blended. Increase speed to medium, and beat 3 minutes. Pour into a greased and floured tube pan. Bake at 325° for 55 minutes. Heat powdered sugar and lemon juice until sugar melts and mixture thickens. Pour over cake.

Cherry Chocolate Cake

1	package chocolate cake mix	5	tablespoons butter or margarine
3	eggs		
1	(21-ounce) can cherry pie filling	⅓	cup milk
1	cup sugar	1	cup (6 ounces) semisweet chocolate morsels

Combine first 3 ingredients. Pour into a greased and floured 13- x 9-inch pan. Bake at 350° for 35 to 40 minutes. Cool. Bring sugar, butter, and milk to a boil in a saucepan. Boil, stirring constantly, 1 minute. Remove from heat, and stir in morsels until melted. Spread over cake.

Peggy's Chocolate Surprise Cake

1 package German chocolate cake mix
½ (14-ounce) can sweetened condensed milk
½ small jar caramel sauce
1 (8-ounce) container frozen whipped topping, thawed
8 chocolate-toffee candy bars, crushed

Prepare cake according to package directions. Cool slightly. Make holes in cake with wooden picks. Dribble in milk and caramel sauce. Let stand 1 hour. Cover with whipped topping; sprinkle with crushed candy.

Chocolate-Raspberry Cheesecake

1½ cups finely crushed cream-filled chocolate sandwich cookies
2 tablespoons butter or margarine, melted
4 (8-ounce) packages cream cheese, softened
1¼ cups sugar
3 eggs
1 cup sour cream
1 teaspoon vanilla extract
1 cup (6 ounces) semisweet chocolate morsels, melted
⅓ cup seedless raspberry jam or preserves

Combine cookie crumbs and butter; press onto bottom of a 9-inch springform pan. Beat 3 packages cream cheese and sugar at medium speed with an electric mixer until well blended. Add eggs, 1 at a time, mixing well. Beat in sour cream and vanilla. Pour mixture over crust. Combine remaining package cream cheese and melted chocolate, mixing well; add jam. Drop jam mixture by rounded tablespoonfuls onto cream cheese layer. Do not swirl. Bake at 325° for 1 hour and 10 minutes. Cool completely before removing sides of pan.

Upside-Down German Chocolate Cake

1 cup pecan pieces
1 cup flaked coconut
1 package German chocolate cake mix
½ cup butter or margarine, melted
1 box powdered sugar
1 (8-ounce) package cream cheese, softened

Sprinkle pecans and coconut into bottom of a greased 13- x 11-inch pan. Prepare cake batter according to package directions. Pour over pecan mixture. Combine butter, sugar, and cream cheese; spoon over cake batter. Bake at 325° for 50 minutes.

Éclair Cake

1	package graham crackers	6	tablespoons cocoa
2	small packages vanilla instant pudding	2	tablespoons vegetable oil
		2	teaspoons light corn syrup
3½	cups milk	2	teaspoons vanilla extract
1	(8-ounce) container frozen whipped topping, thawed	1½	cups powdered sugar
		3	tablespoons milk

Lightly grease a 13- x 9-inch pan. Line bottom of pan with graham crackers. Beat pudding and milk at medium speed with an electric mixer 2 minutes. Add whipped topping, beating until blended. Pour half of pudding mixture over crackers. Add a second layer of crackers, followed by remaining half of pudding mixture. Add a third layer of crackers; Chill 2 hours. Beat cocoa and next 5 ingredients at medium speed with an electric mixer until blended. Spread over cracker layer. Chill 24 hours.

Large Birthday Cake

3	cups sifted all-purpose flour	1½	cups sugar
3½	teaspoons double-acting baking powder	3	eggs
		1½	teaspoons vanilla extract
¾	teaspoon salt	1¼	cups milk
½	cup shortening, softened		

Sift together first 3 ingredients; set aside. Beat shortening, sugar, eggs, and vanilla at medium speed with an electric mixer until creamy. Add flour mixture alternately with milk, beginning and ending with flour mixture. Pour batter into 2 greased 9-inch round cake pans. Bake at 350° for 35 minutes. Spread with desired frosting.

Banana Pudding Cake

1-2	ripe bananas	4	eggs
1	package yellow cake mix	1	cup water
1	package banana cream or vanilla instant pie filling	¼	cup vegetable oil
		½	cup chopped nuts

Mash bananas in a large bowl. Add remaining ingredients, stirring to blend. Beat 2 minutes. Pour into a well-greased and floured tube pan. Bake at 350° for 70 minutes. Cool in pan at least 15 minutes. Remove to a wire rack to cool. Sprinkle with powdered sugar, if desired.

Killer Chocolate Mousse

4	large eggs	2	ounces softened butter
8	ounces chocolate candy bar	1	cup strong coffee
1	ounce unsweetened chocolate	2	tablespoons brandy

Separate whites from yolks and whisk yolks thoroughly. Slowly melt broken up chocolate with the coffee. When all is melted, remove from heat and add softened butter. Blend in egg yolks with the brandy. Beat egg whites until they peak. Stir ⅓ of the beaten egg whites thoroughly into the chocolate mixture, then carefully fold in remaining egg whites. Pour mixture into individual ramekins and set in refrigerator for at least 24 hours.

Chocolate Sheet Cake

1	cup butter or margarine, melted	1	teaspoon ground cinnamon
¼	cup cocoa	½	teaspoon salt
1	cup water	⅓	can sweetened condensed milk
2	cups all-purpose flour	2	eggs
1½	cups packed brown sugar	1	teaspoon vanilla extract
1	teaspoon baking soda		Frosting

Combine first 3 ingredients in a saucepan. Bring to a boil, and remove from heat. Combine flour and next 4 ingredients in a large bowl. Add butter mixture, blending well. Stir in ⅓ can milk, eggs, and vanilla. Pour into a greased 15- x 10-inch jellyroll pan. Bake at 350° for 15 minutes or until cake springs back when touched. Spread with frosting while warm.

Frosting

¼	cup butter or margarine	1	cup powdered sugar
¼	cup cocoa	1	cup chopped nuts
⅔	can sweetened condensed milk		

Melt butter in a small saucepan; stir in cocoa and milk. Stir in powdered sugar and nuts. Spread on warm cake.

Lemon-Lime Pound Cake

1	cup butter or margarine		1	teaspoon lemon extract
½	cup shortening		3	cups all-purpose flour
3	cups sugar		1	(7-ounce) bottle lemon-lime
5	eggs			soft drink

Beat butter, shortening, and sugar at medium speed with an electric mixer until creamy; add eggs, 1 at a time, beating until blended after each addition. Add lemon extract; add flour alternately with soft drink, beginning and ending with flour. Pour into a greased and floured tube pan. Bake at 300° for 1½ hours.

Kentucky Jam Cake

1¾	cups all-purpose flour		1	teaspoon ground cinnamon
1½	cups sugar		1	teaspoon ground nutmeg
1	cup vegetable oil		1	teaspoon allspice
1	cup buttermilk		1	teaspoon vanilla extract
1	cup jam		½	teaspoon ground cloves
3	eggs		½	teaspoon salt
1	teaspoon baking soda		1	cup finely chopped pecans
1	teaspoon baking powder			Buttermilk Icing

Combine first 14 ingredients in a large mixing bowl. Beat, beginning at low speed and increasing to high speed, 8 minutes or until sugar dissolves. Fold in pecans. Pour into 2 greased and floured 8" or 9" round cake pans. Bake at 350° for 40 minutes or until cake pulls away from sides of pans. Cool in pans on a wire rack 20 minutes. Remove from pans, and cool on wire rack. Spread with icing.

Buttermilk Icing

3	cups sugar		2	tablespoons corn syrup
1	cup butter		1	teaspoon baking soda
1	cup buttermilk		1	cup finely chopped pecans

Bring first 5 ingredients to a boil in a 4-quart saucepan, stirring constantly. Insert candy thermometer, and Cook, stirring occasionally, until temperature reaches 238° (soft ball stage). Pour mixture into a large bowl. Beat at high speed with electric mixer until spreading consistency (about 7 minutes). Fold in pecans.

Milky Way Cake

8	(full-size) Milky Way bars	4	eggs
1	cup butter or margarine	1½	cups sugar
1¼	cups buttermilk		Fudge Icing
2½	cups self-rising flour		

Melt candy bars and ½ cup butter in a saucepan over low heat. Set aside to cool. Beat sugar and ½ cup butter at medium speed with an electric mixer until blended. Add eggs, 1 at a time, beating until blended after each addition. Add buttermilk alternately with flour, beating until blended. Add melted candy bars, and beat until blended. Pour batter into a large greased Bundt pan. Bake at 375° for 1 hour and 10 minutes. Cool completely before turning out. Spread with icing.

Fudge Icing

½	cup butter or margarine	6-7	tablespoons milk
3	teaspoons cocoa	1	box powdered sugar
1	teaspoon vanilla extract		

Beat butter at medium speed with an electric mixer until fluffy. Add cocoa, vanilla, and milk, beating until blended. Gradually add powdered sugar; blend until spreading consistency. Spread over cooled cake.

Strawberry Cake

1	package strawberry cake mix	1	(10-ounce) package frozen
1	small box strawberry gelatin		sliced strawberries, thawed
½	cup water		and undrained
½	cup vegetable oil		Icing
4	large eggs		

Beat cake mix, gelatin, water, and oil at medium speed with an electric mixer until blended. Add eggs, 1 at a time, beating well after each. Add three-fourths of strawberries and juice, reserving remainder for Icing; mix well. Pour batter into 2 (9-inch) round cake pans lined with wax paper or 1 (13- x 9-inch) pan lined with wax paper. Bake at 350° for 35 minutes. Cool and spread with Icing.

Icing

½	cup butter or margarine	Reserved strawberries and
1	box powdered sugar	juice
		½ teaspoon vanilla extract

Beat butter and sugar at medium speed with an electric mixer until creamy. Add vanilla and enough berries and juice to reach desired consistency.

Raw Apple Cake

2	cups sugar	½	teaspoon salt
2	eggs	2	teaspoons ground cinnamon
1¼	cups vegetable oil	2	teaspoons vanilla extract
3	cups all-purpose flour	½	cup chopped nuts
1	teaspoon baking soda	3	cups chopped apple

Beat first 3 ingredients with an electric mixer until blended. Add remaining ingredients. Pour into a greased and floured 13- x 9-inch pan. Bake at 350° for 40 minutes.

✓ Fruit Cocktail Cake

1½	cups all-purpose flour	1	egg
1	teaspoon baking soda	1	large can fruit cocktail
½	teaspoon salt	1	cup packed brown sugar
1	cup sugar	½	cup chopped nuts

Combine first 4 ingredients; add egg and fruit. Pour into a greased 13- x 9-inch pan. Combine brown sugar and nuts. Sprinkle over cake. Bake at 375° for 35 minutes.

Chocolate Tea Cake

½	cup shortening	½	cup cocoa
1½	cups sugar	1	teaspoon baking soda
2	eggs	¾	cup all-purpose flour
½	teaspoon salt	¾	cup cake flour
1	cup strong brewed hot tea		

Beat shortening and sugar at medium speed with an electric mixer until creamy. Add eggs and salt, blending until color lightens. Set aside. Place cocoa in a bowl, and stir in tea. Add tea mixture to egg mixture. Add baking soda to remaining tea. Add flours and soda mixture to egg mixture; blend well. Pour batter into 2 greased, wax paper-lined 8-inch cake pans. Bake at 325° for about ½ hour. Cool in pans on a wire rack 10 minutes. Remove from pans, and cool on racks. Frost with white or chocolate icing.

German Chocolate Pound Cake

2 cups sugar	3 cups sifted all-purpose flour
1 cup shortening	½ teaspoon baking soda
4 eggs	1 teaspoon salt
2 teaspoons butter flavoring	1 package sweet German
1 cup buttermilk	chocolate, softened
2 teaspoons vanilla extract	

Beat shortening and sugar at high speed with an electric mixer until creamy. Add eggs and next 3 ingredients. Sift flour, soda, and salt together. Add to sugar mixture. Add chocolate. Blend well. Pour into a greased and floured 9-inch stem angel food or bundt pan. Bake at 300° for 1½ hours. Remove from pan while hot, and place in a tight-fitting container.

Hummingbird Cake

3 cups all-purpose flour	1½ teaspoons vanilla extract
2 cups sugar	1 (8-ounce) can crushed
1 teaspoon baking soda	pineapple
1 teaspoon salt	1 cup chopped pecans
1 teaspoon ground cinnamon	2 cups chopped banana
3 eggs, beaten	Cream cheese frosting
1 cup vegetable oil	½ cup chopped pecans

Combine first 5 ingredients in a large bowl. Add eggs and oil; stir until moistened. Stir in vanilla, pineapple, 1 cup pecans, and banana. Spoon batter into 3 greased 9-inch round cake pans. Bake at 350° for 30 minutes. Cool in pans on wire racks. Remove from pans, and cool on racks. Frost between layers and on top and sides. Sprinkle with ½ cup pecans.

Poor Man's Cake

3 cups all-purpose flour	⅔ cup vegetable oil
2 cups sugar	2 tablespoons vinegar
½ cup cocoa	2 tablespoons vanilla extract
2 teaspoons baking soda	2 cups cold water
1 teaspoon salt	

Combine all ingredients. Pour into a greased and floured tube or Bundt pan. Bake at 350° until a wooden pick inserted in center comes out clean.

Mississippi Mud Cake

1 cup butter or margarine	2 eggs, beaten
3½ tablespoons cocoa	1 teaspoon baking soda
1 cup water	1 teaspoon vanilla extract
2 cups all-purpose flour	½ cup buttermilk
2 cups sugar	Icing

Bring first 3 ingredients to a boil in a saucepan. Sift together flour, sugar, and soda into a large bowl. Add eggs, buttermilk, and vanilla. Add butter mixture. Pour batter into a greased and floured sheet pan. Bake at 350° for 30 to 35 minutes. Top with Icing.

Icing

½ cup butter or margarine	1 box powdered sugar
⅓ cup milk	1 cup chopped nuts
3½ tablespoons cocoa	

Bring first 3 ingredients to a boil in a saucepan. Add remaining ingredients, and pour over warm cake.

Italian Cream Cake

½ cup butter or margarine	1 teaspoon vanilla extract
½ cup shortening	1 (4-ounce) can flaked coconut
2 cups sugar	1 cup chopped nuts
5 egg yolks	5 egg whites, beaten stiff
2 cups all-purpose flour	¼ teaspoon salt
1 teaspoon baking soda	Italian Cream Icing
1 cup buttermilk	

Beat first 3 ingredients at high medium speed with an electric mixer until creamy. Add yolks. Beat well. Combine flour and soda; add to butter mixture alternately with buttermilk. Stir in vanilla. Add coconut and nuts. Fold in egg whites. Pour batter into 3 greased, wax paper-lined 8-inch cake pans. Bake at 350° for 25 minutes. Cool and spread with Italian Cream Icing.

Italian Cream Icing

¼ cup butter or margarine	1 teaspoon vanilla extract
1 box powdered sugar	1 cup chopped nuts
1 (8-ounce) package cream cheese, softened	

Beat butter and cream cheese with electric mixer until creamy. Add sugar, and mix well. Add vanilla, beating until blended. Mix in nuts. Spread between layers and on top and sides of cake.

Chocolate-Mayonnaise Cake

2	cups all-purpose flour	1	cup boiling water
1	cup sugar	1	teaspoon vanilla extract
½	cup cocoa	2	teaspoons baking soda
1	cup mayonnaise		

Combine all ingredients and pour into 13- x 9-inch pan. Bake at 350° for 45 minutes.

Apple Pie Cake

¼	cup shortening	1	teaspoon baking soda
1	cup sugar	2	tablespoons hot water
1	egg	1	teaspoon vanilla extract
1	cup all-purpose flour	½	cup chopped walnuts
1	teaspoon salt	1	(20-ounce) can apples,
1	teaspoon ground cinnamon		drained and diced

Beat shortening and sugar with an electric mixer until creamy. Add egg, and mix well. Add dry ingredients, water, and vanilla. Blend thoroughly. Fold in diced apple and nuts; spread into a greased 8-inch square pan. Bake at 350° for 45 minutes. Serve warm.

Buttermilk Pie ✓

2	cups sugar	½	cup butter, melted
4	eggs	1	teaspoon vanilla extract
2	tablespoons all-purpose flour		Pinch of salt
⅔	cup buttermilk		

Combine all ingredients, blending well. Pour into an unbaked (9-inch) pie shell. Bake at 425° for 10 minutes; reduce temperature to 350°, and bake 30 minutes.

Apricot Nectar Cake

1	package lemon cake mix	1	teaspoon orange extract
½	cup vegetable oil	1	teaspoon lemon extract
¾	cup apricot nectar or orange juice	4	eggs
		1	box orange or lemon gelatin Apricot Glaze

Combine all ingredients; pour into a tube or Bundt pan. Bake at 350° for about 1 hour. Cool in pan 15 minutes. Brush with glaze.

Apricot Glaze

½	cup apricot nectar or orange juice concentrate	1	cup powdered sugar

Mix until smooth.

Four-Layer Chocolate Pie

2	cups all-purpose flour	1	cup sugar
1	cup butter or margarine	2	boxes chocolate instant pudding mix
1	cup pecan pieces	3¼	cups milk
1	(8-ounce) package cream cheese, softened		Frozen whipped topping, thawed
1	cup frozen whipped topping, thawed		

Combine first 3 ingredients; pat into a 13- x 9-inch pan. Bake at 350° for 20 minutes; cool. Beat cream cheese, 1 cup whipped topping, and sugar at medium speed with an electric mixer until fluffy. Spread over prepared crust. Prepare pudding according to package directions, using milk. Pour over cheese layer. Top with whipped topping, and garnish with cherries or grated chocolate. Chill.

Coconut Custard Pie

1	cup flaked coconut	1½	cups hot water
3	eggs	1	teaspoon vanilla extract
1	(14-ounce) can sweetened condensed milk	¼	teaspoon salt
		⅛	teaspoon ground nutmeg

Toast ½ cup coconut; set aside. Beat eggs in a medium bowl. Add milk and next 3 ingredients. Stir in remaining ½ cup coconut. Pour mixture into a 9-inch baked piecrust, cooled. Sprinkle toasted coconut on top. Bake at 425° for 10 minutes. Reduce temperature to 350°. Bake 25 to 30 minutes. Cool and chill.

Sensational Double-Layer Pumpkin Pie

1	(3-ounce) package cream cheese, softened	2	packages vanilla instant pudding mix
1	cup plus 1 tablespoon milk	1	(16-ounce) can pumpkin
1	tablespoon sugar	½	teaspoon ground ginger
1½	cups frozen whipped topping, thawed	1	teaspoon ground cinnamon
1	graham cracker piecrust	¼	teaspoon ground cloves

Whisk together cream cheese, 1 tablespoon milk, and sugar until smooth. Stir in whipped topping. Spread mixture on bottom of piecrust. Whisk together 1 cup milk and pudding mix until well blended. Let pudding mixture stand 3 minutes. Stir pumpkin and spices into pudding mixture. Spread over cream cheese layer. Chill at least 2 hours. Dollop with whipped topping.

Cranberry-Peach Pie

1	(29-ounce) can peach slices, undrained	3	tablespoons cornstarch
3	cups fresh cranberries	¼	cup chopped almonds, toasted
1½	cups sugar		Pastry for 2-crust pie

Drain peaches, reserving 1 cup syrup. Cut peaches into chunks, and set aside. Combine cranberries and reserved peach syrup in a saucepan; cook over medium heat until cranberry skins pop. Combine sugar and cornstarch; add to cranberry mixture. Cook, stirring constantly, until mixture thickens and bubbles. Remove from heat. Stir in peaches and almonds. Fit 1 pastry into a 9-inch pie plate. Pour cranberry mixture into pastry. Arrange remaining pastry in a lattice design over top. Crimp edges to seal. Bake at 400° for 30 to 45 minutes.

'No Peekee' Apple Pie

1½ cups all-purpose flour	½ teaspoon ground nutmeg
1½ teaspoons sugar	1 teaspoon ground cinnamon
1 teaspoon salt	4 cups sliced apple
½ cup vegetable oil	½ cup all-purpose flour
2 tablespoons milk	½ cup butter or margarine
½ cup sugar	½ cup sugar
2 tablespoons all-purpose flour	

Combine first 5 ingredients. Pat into bottom and up sides of a 9-inch pie plate. (Do not roll out.) Set crust aside. Combine ½ cup sugar, 2 tablespoons flour, nutmeg, and cinnamon; toss with apple. Spoon apple mixture into crust. Combine remaining ingredients, and sprinkle over pie. Place in a large paper bag, and seal or fold down. Bake at 350° for 1 hour and 45 minutes. No peeking!

Mock Apple Pie

Pastry for 2-crust pie	2 tablespoons lemon juice
36 buttery round crackers, coarsely broken	Grated rind of 1 lemon
2 cups water	2 tablespoons butter or margarine
2 cups sugar	½ teaspoons ground cinnamon
2 teaspoons cream of tartar	

Fit 1 piecrust into a pie plate. Sprinkle crackers into bottom. Bring water, sugar, and cream of tartar to a boil in a saucepan over high heat. Reduce heat, and simmer 15 minutes. Add lemon juice and rind; cool. Pour sugar mixture over crackers, and dot with butter. Sprinkle with cinnamon, and cover with remaining crust. Bake at 425° for 30 to 35 minutes.

Key Lime Pie

6 egg yolks	1 (8-ounce) bottle lime juice concentrate
2 (14-ounce) cans sweetened condensed milk	Liquid yellow food coloring
	1 baked (9-inch) pie shell

Beat first 4 ingredients at medium speed with an electric mixer. Pour into a baked 9-inch pie shell. Bake at 325° for 40 minutes. Cool and chill. Top with whipped cream and lime slices.

Chess Pie

5 tablespoons melted butter or margarine	1 teaspoon vanilla extract
1½ cups sugar	3 eggs, separated
3 tablespoons vinegar	½ teaspoon ground nutmeg

Combine butter and sugar in a medium bowl. Add vinegar, vanilla, and egg yolks. Stir until blended. Beat egg whites until soft peaks form; add to butter mixture. Pour into unbaked (9-inch) pie shell. Sprinkle with nutmeg. Bake at 275° for 40 minutes or until set.

Caramel Candy Pie

25-30 caramel candies	Pinch of salt
2 cups milk, divided	1 teaspoon vanilla
3 egg yolks	1 baked (9-inch) pie shell
2 teaspoons cornstarch	

Melt caramels in 1 cup milk in top of a double boiler. Beat egg yolks well; combine with remaining 1 cup milk and cornstarch in a small bowl. Pour melted caramels into bowl with yolk mixture. Add salt. Return to double boiler. Cook over medium-low heat, stirring constantly, until thick. Add vanilla, and pour into pie shell. Top with whipped cream.

Cherry Cheese Pie

1 (8-ounce) package cream cheese, softened	⅓ cup lemon juice
1 (14-ounce) can sweetened condensed milk	1 (21-ounce) can cherry pie filling, chilled
1 teaspoon vanilla extract	1 (9-inch) graham cracker crust

Beat cream cheese at medium speed with an electric mixer until fluffy. Gradually beat in milk until smooth. Stir in lemon juice and vanilla. Pour into crust. Chill 3 hours or until set. Top with pie filling just before serving. Chill leftovers.

Esther Latzke's Lemon Pie

4   eggs
¼   cup lemon juice
    Grated rind of 1 lemon

3   tablespoons water
1   cup sugar
    Pastry for 1 piecrust

Separate eggs, placing whites in a mixing bowl and yolks in top of a double boiler. Beat yolks with electric mixer until thick. Add lemon juice and rind, water, and ½ cup sugar. Cook over boiling water, stirring constantly, until thick. Remove from heat. Beat egg whites until stiff; add remaining ½ cup sugar, and beat until soft, fine meringue forms. Fold half of meringue into warm yolk mixture. Pour into baked piecrust. Make a wreath around edge of pie with remaining meringue. Set pie in oven at 325° just long enough to lightly brown meringue.

Little Pecan Pies

4   ounces cream cheese,
    softened
½   cup butter or margarine,
    softened
1   cup all-purpose flour
2   eggs

2   tablespoons butter or
    margarine
2   teaspoons vanilla extract
1   cup chopped pecans
    Dash of salt
1½ cups packed brown sugar

Beat cream cheese and butter or margarine until fluffy; stir in flour. Chill 1 hour. Roll cream cheese mixture into 22 to 24 balls. Press into muffin pans, forming shells. Combine remaining ingredients, and fill. Bake at 325° for 15 minutes or until crust is golden.

Rhubarb Custard Pie

2¼ cups finely chopped rhubarb
1½ cups sugar
1½ tablespoons all-purpose flour
¼   teaspoon ground nutmeg
1   teaspoon vanilla extract

⅛   teaspoon salt
3   eggs
3   tablespoons butter or
    margarine, melted
1   unbaked (9-inch) pie shell

Beat eggs with an electric mixer 5 minutes. Gradually add sugar, beating during each addition. Add flour, nutmeg, and salt while beating. Pour into pie shell. Bake 350° for 1 hour.

About 3 stalks rhubarb equals 2¼ cups chopped.

Easy Pecan Pie

3   eggs, lightly beaten
1   cup sugar
1   cup light or dark corn syrup
1   tablespoon butter or
    margarine, melted

1   teaspoon vanilla extract
1   cup pecan halves
1   unbaked (9-inch) piecrust

Stir together first 5 ingredients. Stir in pecans. Pour into piecrust. Bake at 350° for 50 to 60 minutes or until knife inserted halfway between center and edge comes out clean.

Cottage Pudding

¾   cup packed brown sugar
2   tablespoons butter or
    margarine
2   teaspoons baking powder
1¼ cups all-purpose flour
1   teaspoon salt
½   cup milk

¾   cup raisins
1   teaspoon vanilla extract
1   cup packed brown sugar
1   tablespoon butter or
    margarine
¼   teaspoon ground nutmeg
2½ cups boiling water

Beat butter and brown sugar at medium speed with an electric mixer until creamy. Add dry ingredients alternately with milk, beating until smooth. Stir in raisins and vanilla; spread batter into a greased 9-inch square pan. Combine 1 cup brown sugar, 1 tablespoon butter, and nutmeg in a large bowl. Stir in water. Pour mixture over batter (do not stir). Bake at 375° for 40 minutes.

Cookies-and-Cream Dessert

1   (16-ounce) package chocolate
    sandwich cookies, crushed
1   (8-ounce) package cream
    cheese, softened
½   cup butter or margarine,
    softened
1   cup powdered sugar

1   (8-ounce) container frozen
    whipped topping, thawed
2   small boxes vanilla instant
    pudding mix
3   cups milk
1   teaspoon vanilla extract

Press half of cookie crumbs into bottom of a 13- x 9-inch baking dish. Mix cream cheese and butter until smooth. Stir in powdered sugar. Fold in whipped topping. Set aside. Combine pudding mix, milk, and vanilla. Fold cream cheese mixture into pudding mixture. Pour over cookie crumbs. Sprinkle remaining crumbs over top. Chill until set.

Layered Dessert

1½ cups all-purpose flour
¾ cup butter or margarine
¾ cup chopped nuts
1 (8-ounce) package cream cheese
1 (8-ounce) container frozen whipped topping, thawed
1 cup powdered sugar
2 boxes vanilla or chocolate instant pudding mix
3 cups milk
1 teaspoon vanilla extract

Combine first 3 ingredients; pat into bottom of a 13- x 9-inch pan. Bake at 350° for 15 minutes. Cool. Beat cream cheese, whipped topping, and powdered sugar with an electric mixer 2 minutes; spread over baked crust. Beat pudding mix, milk, and vanilla 2 minutes; spread over cream cheese layer. Chill. Top with whipped topping and nuts.

Chocolate Torte

1 cup all-purpose flour
½ cup butter or margarine
½ cup chopped walnuts
1 (8-ounce) package cream cheese, softened
1 cup powdered sugar
1 (12-ounce) container frozen whipped topping, thawed
1 large box chocolate instant pudding mix

Cut flour and butter with a fork until crumbly. Add walnuts. Pat mixture into a 13- x 9-inch pan. Bake at 375° for 15 minutes. Cool. Beat cream cheese until creamy; add powdered sugar. Fold in whipped topping. Prepare pudding according to package directions; allow to set. Spoon cream cheese mixture onto prepared crust, then spread evenly. Top with pudding. Spread with additional whipped topping.

Rice Pudding

1 pound long-grain rice
2 cups sugar
1 large box raisins
1-2 tablespoons vanilla extract
1 quart whole milk
1 large can cream
4 eggs

Cook rice according to package directions; set aside. Cook milk, cream, eggs, sugar, and vanilla in a saucepan over medium-low heat until mixture thickens. Add rice. Cook to desired consistency. Pudding will thicken as it cools.

Lemon Charlotte Russe

3 packages ladyfingers
1 small can frozen lemonade, thawed
1 can sweetened condensed milk
Juice of 1 lemon
Grated rind of ½ lemon

Dash of liquid yellow food coloring
2 (8-ounce) containers frozen whipped topping, thawed
2 cups whipping cream, whipped

Line sides and bottom of a springform pan with ladyfingers. Combine lemon juice, lemonade, milk, rind, and food coloring. Fold in 1 container whipped topping. Pour half of mixture over ladyfingers. Cover with more ladyfingers. Repeat procedure. Spread remaining container whipped topping over top. Spread with whipped cream. Garnish with lemon twists and other fruit.

Sugar Plum Pudding

2 cups all-purpose flour
1½ teaspoons baking soda
½ teaspoon salt
3 eggs
1 jar plum baby food
1 teaspoon ground nutmeg
1 teaspoon allspice
1 teaspoon ground cinnamon
1½ cups sugar

2½ teaspoons baking powder
¾ cup vegetable oil
1 cup buttermilk
1 cup chopped nuts
1 cup sugar
1 tablespoon corn syrup
1 teaspoon vanilla extract
½ cup buttermilk
½ cup butter or margarine

Combine first 13 ingredients. Bake in a greased pan at 325° for 40 minutes. Bring 1 cup sugar, corn syrup, and remaining ingredients to a boil in a saucepan. Pour over pudding.

Lemon Dessert

1 small box lemon gelatin
1¾ cups hot water
¼ cup lemon juice
1 cup sugar

1 large can evaporated milk, chilled at least 8 hours
16 graham crackers

Dissolve gelatin in hot water until consistency of beaten egg white. Beat until light and fluffy; add lemon juice and sugar. Whip milk, and fold into gelatin mixture. Crush crackers, and sprinkle into a large cake pan. Pour lemon mixture over top. Chill at least 8 hours, or until set.

Party Fruit Kuchen

1   (1-pound, 14-ounce) can apricot halves
1   (9-inch) yellow cake layer, baked
4   large canned pear halves, drained

10-12   maraschino cherries
¼   cup butter or margarine
½   cup packed light brown sugar
½   cup chopped pecans
    Whipped topping

Drain apricots, reserving liquid. Place cake on a serving plate. Prick with fork. Spoon ¼ cup apricot juice over cake. Alternate apricots and pears on top of cake, forming pattern. Decorate with cherries. Melt butter in a saucepan; remove from heat, and stir in brown sugar. Spread side of cake and edges around fruit with half of butter mixture. Press pecans into buttered spaces. Add 2 tablespoons remaining apricot juice to remaining butter mixture. Cook, stirring often, until thoroughly heated. Pour over cake. Serve with whipped topping.

Double Chocolate Layer Bars

1   package extra-moist German chocolate cake mix
1   egg
½   cup butter or margarine, melted
2   cups flaked coconut

1   cup (6 ounces) semisweet chocolate morsels
½   cup chopped nuts
1   (14-ounce) can sweetened condensed milk

Combine cake mix, egg, and butter. Press firmly into bottom of a 13- x 9-inch baking dish. Sprinkle coconut over top; sprinkle with morsels and nuts. Cover with milk. Bake at 350° for 30 minutes. Cool and cut into bars. Chill in airtight container to store.

Microwave Caramel Corn

    Popcorn
½   cup butter or margarine
¼   cup corn syrup

1   cup packed brown sugar
½   teaspoon salt
½   teaspoon baking soda

Prepare 10 cups popcorn; place into a paper bag greased with cooking spray. In a large microwave-safe bowl, combine butter, corn syrup, brown sugar, and salt. Microwave on HIGH until mixture boils 2 minutes. Stir in baking soda. Quickly pour over popcorn. Fold bag down, and microwave on HIGH 1½ minutes. Shake well, and cook 30 seconds longer.

Lemon Lush

1½ cups all-purpose flour	1 cup frozen whipped topping, thawed
¾ cup butter or margarine	
1½ cups ground walnuts	2 small boxes lemon (or chocolate) instant pudding mix
1 (8-ounce) package cream cheese, softened	
1 cup powdered sugar	3 cups cold milk
1 teaspoon vanilla extract	

Cut flour, butter, and walnuts with a pastry blender until crumbly. Pat into bottom of a 13- x 9-inch baking dish. Bake at 350° for 30 minutes. Cool. Mix cream cheese, powdered sugar, vanilla, and whipped topping. Spread over cooled crust. Chill. Combine pudding mix and milk. As soon as pudding thickens, pour over cream cheese layer. Top with whipped topping, and sprinkle with chopped walnuts.

You may add ½ cup lemon juice to pudding and decrease milk by ½ cup.

Crustless Peach Cobbler

1 cup sugar	1 (16-ounce) can peaches, undrained
1 cup self-rising flour	
¾ cup milk	Cinnamon-sugar
¼ cup butter or margarine	

Combine sugar, flour, and milk. Melt butter in a shallow baking dish; top with flour mixture. Do not stir. Top evenly with peaches and juice. Bake at 350° for 40 minutes. Sprinkle with cinnamon-sugar and bake for 10 minutes longer. Serve with ice cream.

Fresh Peach Crumble

5 cups peeled, sliced peaches	⅛ teaspoon ground cinnamon
2 tablespoons sugar	¼ cup butter or margarine, cut up
1 tablespoon lemon juice	
½ cup all-purpose flour	½ cup regular or quick oats
½ cup packed light brown sugar	

Toss peaches with sugar and lemon juice. Spread evenly in a 2-quart baking dish. Combine flour, brown sugar, and cinnamon; cut in butter until crumbly. Add oats. Sprinkle over peach mixture. Bake at 400° for 30 minutes or until browned and bubbly.

Quick Cobbler

1½ cups sugar
1   cup all-purpose flour
1   teaspoon baking powder

1   egg
1   large can fruit

Combine first 4 ingredients. Heat fruit to boiling, and place in a 9-inch square pan. Sprinkle sugar mixture over fruit. Bake at 425° for 20 to 25 minutes or until browned.

Snow Cream

1   large can sweetened
    condensed milk
1   cup sugar

2   teaspoons vanilla extract
    Snow

Combine first 3 ingredients in a large bowl. Add snow until desired thickness. Eat like ice cream.

Homemade Vanilla Ice Cream

½   gallon sweet milk
3   eggs, beaten
1½ cups sugar

1   can sweetened condensed
    milk
1   teaspoon vanilla extract

Combine all ingredients, stirring well. Freeze according to ice-cream freezer directions.

Mexican Chocolate Ice Cream

3   eggs
1   cup sugar
2   quarts half-and-half
1   (16-ounce) can chocolate
    syrup

½   teaspoon ground cinnamon
1   tablespoon vanilla extract
¼   teaspoon almond extract

Beat eggs at medium speed with an electric mixer until frothy. Gradually add sugar, beating until thick. Heat half-and-half in a 3-quart saucepan over low heat until hot. Gradually add one-fourth hot cream into egg mixture. Add egg mixture to remaining hot cream. Cook over low heat, stirring constantly, until slightly thickened. Remove from heat; stir in chocolate, cinnamon, and extracts. Chill, and freeze according to ice-cream freezer directions.

Toffee Ice Cream Dessert

1¼ cups chocolate wafer crumbs
¼ cup melted butter or margarine
12 small toffee-chocolate candy bars
½ gallon vanilla or French vanilla ice cream, softened
¼ cup butter or margarine
1 cup (6 ounces) semisweet chocolate morsels
1 cup powdered sugar
1 small can evaporated milk
1 teaspoon vanilla extract

Combine wafer crumbs and melted butter. Pat into a 13- x 9-inch pan; place in freezer until hardened. Process toffee bars in a food processor; combine with ice cream in a large bowl. Spoon ice cream mixture into crust, and freeze until firm. Melt remaining ¼ cup butter in a saucepan; add morsels, stirring until smooth. Add powdered sugar and milk. Cook about 8 minutes or until thickened. Add vanilla. Cool completely, and spread over ice cream mixture. Return to freezer until firm.

Peach Cobbler

1¾ cups all-purpose flour
1 teaspoon salt
½ cup shortening
⅓ cup milk
3 cups peach slices
1 tablespoon all-purpose flour
1¼ cups sugar
¼ teaspoon ground cinnamon
½ cup butter or margarine, melted

Combine first 4 ingredients, blending with a pastry blender until crumbly. Press into bottom of a baking dish. Combine peaches and next 3 ingredients; pour over crust. Use remaining crust mixture to layer lattice design over peach mixture. Drizzle butter over top. Bake at 350° for 40 to 45 minutes.

You may substitute another fruit for peaches.

Frozen Dessert

1 egg white
Dash of salt
¼ cup sugar
1 cup chopped pecans
1 pint strawberry ice cream, softened
1 pint vanilla ice cream, softened

Beat egg white and salt with an electric mixer until stiff. Gradually add sugar. Fold in nuts. Press into a greased 9-inch pie plate; prick with a fork. Bake at 400° for 11 minutes. Combine ice creams. Spread over egg mixture, and freeze.

Chocolate-Raspberry Roulade

½	ounce vanilla	2	teaspoons baking powder
1½	ounces chocolate-raspberry	13	egg whites
	flavoring	1	tablespoon water
½	cup water	½	teaspoon cream of tartar
½	cup cocoa	1	tablespoon cornstarch
1	cup powdered sugar		Raspberry preserves
¾	cup cake flour		(no-sugar kind)
¼	teaspoon salt		Chocolate mousse

Beat first 8 ingredients in a large bowl. Whip eggs whites and next 3 ingredients. Fold mixtures together. Divide into 2 portions, and spread into 2 (15- x10-inch) jellyroll pans lined with greased parchment paper. Bake at 350° for 13 minutes. Cool 15 minutes. Gently roll up. Cool completely. Unroll, and spread each sheet with 4 to 5 ounces of no-sugar-added raspberry preserves. Spread chocolate mousse (your favorite kind) over preserves. Roll gently, and place in container to hold shape. Freeze. Cut each roll while frozen into 8 slices. Garnish, if desired.

Pineapple-Cookie Dessert

36	cream-filled chocolate	¼	cup milk
	sandwich cookies	1	(20-ounce) can crushed
¼	cup butter or margarine,		pineapple, drained
	melted	1	(8-ounce) container frozen
25	large marshmallows		whipped topping, thawed

Crush 24 cookies, and stir into melted butter. Pat into bottom and up sides of a pie plate. Cook marshmallows and milk in a saucepan until marshmallows melt. Cool and add pineapple and whipped topping. Pour into crust. Crush remaining cookies, and sprinkle over top of pie. Chill until ready to serve.

Boil Cookies

½	cup butter or margarine	1	teaspoon vanilla extract
2	cups sugar	1	cup raisins
3	tablespoons cocoa	½	cup crunchy peanut butter
½	cup milk	3	cups quick-cooking oats

Bring first 4 ingredients to a boil in a saucepan. Boil 1 minute. Remove from heat, and add remaining ingredients. Drop by teaspoonfuls onto aluminum foil to cool.

Spring Fantasy Roll

2 cups (12 ounces) semisweet chocolate morsels
½ cup butter or margarine
2 eggs
2 cups powdered sugar
1 teaspoon vanilla extract

1 (10½-ounce) package plus 1½ cups multicolored marshmallows
1 cup chopped nuts
6 ounces flaked coconut

Melt morsels and butter in a saucepan over low heat; add eggs, powdered sugar, and vanilla. Cool. Add marshmallows and nuts. Divide coconut onto 4 squares aluminum foil. Roll one-fourth of chocolate mixture onto each to form rolls. Chill and slice.

Fruit Shortbread Cookies

1 cup butter or shortening
¾ cup sugar
1½ cups all-purpose flour
1 can fruit pie filling (any flavor)

¼ cup sugar
2 tablespoons ground cinnamon

Beat butter and ¾ cup sugar at high speed with an electric mixer until creamy. Add flour; mix until crumbly. Press mixture into a greased pan. Bake at 350° for 20 minutes or until golden. Cool 2 hours. Spread with fruit filling. Combine ¼ cup sugar and cinnamon; sprinkle over fruit.

Jean's Bars

¾ cup plus ½ cup butter or margarine, divided
1½ cups all-purpose flour
⅜ cup sugar
1 cup graham cracker crumbs
½ cup semisweet chocolate morsels

½ cup chopped nuts
1 teaspoon baking powder
¼ teaspoon salt
1 can sweetened condensed milk
1½ cups powdered sugar
1 teaspoon vanilla extract

Beat ¾ cup butter, flour, and sugar until blended. Press into an ungreased 13- x 9-inch pan. Bake at 375° for 10 minutes. Cool 10 minutes. Combine cracker crumbs and next 5 ingredients; spread over crust. Bake 15 to 20 minutes or until golden brown. Cool. Beat powdered sugar, ½ cup butter, and vanilla until creamy. Spread over bars.

Sugar Cookies

½ cup butter or margarine
½ cup sugar
½ cup powdered sugar
1 egg
½ cup vegetable oil

1 teaspoon vanilla extract
2 cups all-purpose flour
½ teaspoon baking soda
½ teaspoon cream of tartar

Beat butter and sugars at medium speed with an electric mixer until creamy. Add egg, oil, and vanilla, blending well. Combine flour, soda, and cream of tartar. Beat into butter mixture. Cover and chill dough ½ hour. Shape into balls, and roll in sugar. Flatten with bottom of a glass. Bake at 350° for 8 to 10 minutes.

Oatmeal Pie

½ cup butter or margarine, melted
½ cup packed brown sugar
1 cup light corn syrup

2 eggs
1 teaspoon vanilla extract
1 cup quick-cooking oats
1 (9-inch) unbaked pie shell

Combine all ingredients, and pour into pie shell. Bake at 350° for 45 to 50 minutes. Don't overbake.

Party Time Cookies

1½ cups all-purpose flour
½ cup cocoa
¼ teaspoon salt
¼ teaspoon baking powder
¼ teaspoon baking soda
½ cup butter or margarine, softened
1 cup sugar

1 egg
1½ teaspoons vanilla extract
1 (10-ounce) jar maraschino cherries, undrained
1 cup (6 ounces) semisweet chocolate morsels
½ cup sweetened condensed milk

Combine first 5 ingredients in a bowl; set aside. In a large bowl, beat butter and sugar until creamy; add eggs and vanilla, beating well. Gradually add dry ingredients to butter mixture, and beat until blended. Shape into 1-inch balls, and place on ungreased cookie sheets. Press down in center with your thumb or a spoon handle. Place a cherry in each center. Cook morsels and milk in a saucepan over low heat until chocolate melts. Stir in 4 teaspoons cherry liquid. Spoon about 1 teaspoon chocolate mixture over each cherry, spreading to cover cherry. Bake at 350° for 10 minutes. Remove to wire racks to cool.

Easy Filled Cookies

1 cup butter or margarine	½ teaspoon baking powder
2 cups packed brown sugar	⅛ teaspoon ground cinnamon
2 eggs	½ cup milk
3½ cups all-purpose flour	1 teaspoon vanilla extract
½ teaspoon salt	Raisin-Spice Filling
1 teaspoon baking soda	Mincemeat-Orange Filling

Cream butter and brown sugar; add eggs, blending thoroughly. Stir in remaining ingredients. Drop by teaspoonfuls onto greased cookie sheets. With a spoon, form a well in each mound, and place 1 teaspoon cooled filling in each well. Drop another small portion batter over filling. Bake at 375° for 12 to 15 minutes.

Raisin-Spice Filling

2 cups raisins	½ teaspoon cloves
½ cup water	1 tablespoon cornstarch
½ cup sugar	

Combine all ingredients in a saucepan. Cook, stirring often, until thickened.

Mincemeat Filling

2 cups mincemeat	2 tablespoons grated orange rind

Combine mincemeat and rind.

Peanut Butter Kiss Cookies

½ cup peanut butter	1⅓ cups all-purpose flour
½ cup butter or margarine	1 teaspoon baking soda
½ cup sugar	½ teaspoon salt
½ cup packed brown sugar	¼ cup sugar
1 teaspoon vanilla extract	36 milk chocolate kisses
1 egg	

Beat first 4 ingredients with an electric mixer until creamy. Beat in egg and vanilla. In another bowl, combine flour, soda, and salt; gradually add to peanut butter mixture, beating well. Place ¼ cup sugar into a small bowl. Shape dough into 1-inch balls, and roll in sugar to coat. Place on greased cookie sheets. Bake at 350° for 10 minutes. Remove from oven, and quickly press a kiss into each cookie. Bake 3 to 5 more minutes or until lightly browned. Cool on wire racks.

Whaddayacallits

1 cup sugar
1 cup light corn syrup
1 cup peanut butter
5 cups crisp rice cereal

1 cup (6 ounces) semisweet chocolate morsels
1 cup (6 ounces) butterscotch or peanut butter morsels

Bring sugar and syrup to a boil in a saucepan. Add peanut butter, and stir. Stir in cereal, and spread in a 13- x 9-inch pan. Combine morsels, and sprinkle over top. Cut into bars.

Poor Man's Cookies

1 cup raisins
2 cups water
½ cup shortening
1 cup sugar
2 cups all-purpose flour

1 teaspoon each baking soda, ground cinnamon, and nutmeg
½ teaspoon each allspice, cloves, and salt
1 egg

Cook raisins and water in a saucepan until water is reduced to 1 cup. Add shortening and sugar. Remove from heat; cool. Add dry ingredients, mixing well. Blend in egg. Pour onto a greased cookie sheet. Bake at 350° for 20 to 25 minutes. Frost with powdered sugar frosting while warm. Cut when cool.

Oatmeal Drop Cookies

2 eggs
¾ cup vegetable oil
½ cup milk
1 cup honey
1½ teaspoons vanilla extract
2½ cups all-purpose flour
1 teaspoon salt
1 teaspoon baking soda

1½ teaspoons ground cinnamon
1 teaspoon allspice
2 cups rolled oats
1 cup raisins
1 cup candied mixed fruit, chopped
1 cup chopped nuts

Beat eggs; add oil and next 3 ingredients, blending well. Combine flour and next 4 ingredients; stir oats, fruit, and nuts into flour mixture. Add to egg mixture, blending well. Drop by teaspoonfuls onto greased cookie sheets. Bake at 350° for 10 to 12 minutes.

Chocolate Chip Cookies

2	cups plus 4 tablespoons flour	1	package vanilla or chocolate
1	teaspoon baking soda		instant pudding mix
1	cup butter or margarine	2	eggs
½	cup packed brown sugar	2	cups (12 ounces) semisweet
½	cup sugar		chocolate morsels
1	teaspoon vanilla extract	½	cup chopped nuts

Combine flour and soda; set aside. Cream butter and next 4 ingredients. Beat in eggs; gradually beat in flour mixture. Stir in morsels and nuts. (Dough will be stiff.) Drop by teaspoonfuls onto ungreased cookie sheets. Bake at 350° for 8 to 10 minutes.

Nut Bars

½	cup butter or margarine	½	cup light corn syrup
1½	cups all-purpose flour	2	tablespoons butter or
½	teaspoon salt		margarine
¾	cup sugar	1	tablespoon water
1	cup (6 ounces) butterscotch morsels	1	(12½-ounce) can mixed nuts

Cut butter into next 3 ingredients with a pastry blender until crumbly. Pat into a 13- x 9-inch pan. Bake at 350° for 10 minutes. Cook morsels and next 3 ingredients in a saucepan over low heat until morsels melt. Pour over crust. Top with nuts. Bake at 350° for 10 minutes.

Hazelnut Sandies

1	cup butter, softened	1	teaspoon vanilla extract
2¼	cups all-purpose flour	¾	cup finely chopped hazelnuts
⅓	cup sugar	40	whole hazelnuts
1	tablespoon water	¾	cup sifted powdered sugar

Beat butter until creamy. Add 2 cups flour, sugar, water, and vanilla; beat until blended. Stir in remaining flour and chopped nuts. Shape 2 teaspoons dough around each hazelnut. Place on ungreased cookie sheets. Bake at 325° for 20 minutes or until bottoms are lightly browned. Cool on a wire rack. Gently roll cookies in powdered sugar.

Chocolate Drop Cookies

2	(1-ounce) squares unsweetened chocolate	1	teaspoon vanilla extract
½	cup shortening	1½	cups all-purpose flour
1	cup packed brown sugar	¼	teaspoon salt
1	egg	1	teaspoon baking powder
½	cup milk	½	cup nuts, chopped

Melt chocolate and shortening in a saucepan over low heat. Add sugar, egg, milk, and vanilla. Add dry ingredients, and let stand 10 minutes. Drop by teaspoonfuls onto greased cookie sheets. Bake at 375° for 10 minutes. Frost, if desired.

Chocolate-Oatmeal Cookies

2	cups sugar	1	teaspoon vanilla extract
¼	cup cocoa		Pinch of salt
½	cup milk	3	cups regular or quick-cooking oats
½	cup butter or margarine		
½	cup peanut butter		

Bring first 4 ingredients to a boil in a saucepan. Remove from heat, and add peanut butter, vanilla, and salt. Let stand 1 minute; stir in oats. Drop by teaspoonfuls onto wax paper.

Chewy Chocolate Cookies

2	cups sugar	4	eggs
½	cup butter or margarine, melted	2	teaspoons vanilla extract
4	(1-ounce) squares unsweetened chocolate, melted	2	cups all-purpose flour
		2	teaspoons baking powder
		¾	teaspoon salt
		¾	cup powdered sugar

Beat first 3 ingredients with an electric mixer until smooth. Add eggs, 1 at a time, beating until well blended. Beat in vanilla. Combine flour, baking powder, and salt; gradually add to butter mixture, beating well after each addition. Cover and chill 2 hours or overnight. Place powdered sugar into a bowl. Drop dough by teaspoonfuls into powdered sugar, coating each. Shape into balls. Place on greased cookie sheets. Bake at 350° for 12 to 14 minutes. Cool on wire racks.

Molasses Cookies

2	cups all-purpose flour	¼	teaspoon ground cloves
1	cup sugar	¼	teaspoon salt
2	teaspoons baking powder	¾	cup butter or margarine
1	teaspoon ground ginger	¼	cup molasses
2	teaspoons ground cinnamon	1	egg, beaten
¼	teaspoon ground nutmeg	1	teaspoon vanilla extract

Combine dry ingredients in a bowl. Melt butter in a saucepan over low heat; remove from heat, and stir in molasses. Cool. Add egg and vanilla to molasses mixture. Fold into dry ingredients, and chill. Shape dough into 1-inch balls, and place on ungreased cookie sheets. Bake at 350° for 10 to 12 minutes.

Skillet Cookies

2	eggs	1	cup chopped nuts
1	cup sugar	1	cup dates
1	tablespoon butter or margarine	2	cups crisp rice cereal
			Coconut or sugar

Beat eggs; add sugar, butter, and dates. Cook in a heavy skillet over medium heat, stirring constantly, until mixture leaves sides of pan and turns light brown. Stir in nuts and cereal. Remove from heat. With greased hands, roll mixture into small balls. Roll in coconut.

Peanut Butter Temptations

1	cup butter or margarine, softened	1	teaspoon vanilla extract
1	cup peanut butter	2⅔	cups all-purpose flour
1	cup sugar	1½	teaspoons baking soda
1	cup packed brown sugar	1	teaspoon salt
2	eggs	60	miniature peanut butter cups

Beat first 6 ingredients at medium speed with an electric mixer until blended. Add flour, soda, and salt, beating until blended. Shape into 1½-inch balls. Place in muffin pans. Bake at 375° for 8 to 10 minutes or until lightly browned. Remove from oven; press 1 peanut butter cup into center of each cookie while still hot. Cool in pans on wire rack. Remove to wire racks to cool completely.

Oatmeal-Raisin Cookies

1 cup butter or margarine, softened
1 cup packed brown sugar
½ cup sugar
2 eggs
1 teaspoon vanilla extract
1½ cups all-purpose flour

1 teaspoon baking soda
1 teaspoon ground cinnamon
½ teaspoon salt
3 cups regular or quick-cooking oats
1 cups raisins

Beat butter and sugars at medium speed with an electric mixer until creamy. Add eggs and vanilla; beat well. Combine flour and next 3 ingredients; add to butter mixture, beating until blended. Stir in oats and raisins. Drop by rounded tablespoonfuls onto ungreased cookie sheets. Bake at 350° for 10 to 12 minutes or until golden brown. Cool 1 minute on cookie sheets; remove to wire rack to cool completely.

Rolled Christmas Cookies

2½ cups all-purpose flour
¼ teaspoon salt
¾ cup butter or margarine

1½ cups sugar
1 egg
2 teaspoons vanilla extract

Sift flour and salt together. Beat butter and sugar at high speed with an electric mixer until creamy. Add egg and vanilla. Stir in dry ingredients. Mix well. Cover and chill 3 hours. Roll out, and cut with cookie cutters. Place 1 inch apart on ungreased baking sheets. Bake at 350° for about 8 minutes. Cook on wire racks, and decorate with buttercream icing and sprinkles.

Best-of-Show Peanut Butter Cookies

1 cup shortening
1 cup sugar
1 cup packed brown sugar
1 teaspoon vanilla extract
2 eggs, beaten

1 cup peanut butter
2 cups all-purpose flour
2 teaspoons baking soda
1 teaspoon salt

Beat first 4 ingredients at medium speed with an electric mixer until creamed. Add eggs, and beat well. Add peanut butter. Sift dry ingredients, and add to shortening mixture. Drop by teaspoonfuls onto greased baking sheets. Press with a floured fork to make crisscross pattern. Bake at 350° for 10 minutes.

Chruseiki

4 eggs	1 tablespoon vanilla extract
1 teaspoon salt	4 cups all-purpose flour
1 cup powdered sugar	Vegetable oil
½ cup butter or margarine	

Beat eggs; add salt, powdered sugar, butter and vanilla. Fold in flour, and knead dough until it blisters. Turn out onto a floured surface, and roll very thin. Cut into 1-inch strips on diagonal. Cut a ½-inch slit crosswise in middle of each strip. Pull 1 end through slit, forming a bow shape. Cook in a skillet in hot oil over medium heat until golden brown. Drain on paper towels, and sprinkle with powdered sugar.

Never-Fail Fudge

2½ cups sugar	¼ teaspoon salt
¾ cup evaporated milk	1 cup (6 ounces) semisweet chocolate morsels
16 large or 160 miniature marshmallows, or 1 cup marshmallow cream	1 cup chopped nuts
¼ cup butter or margarine	1 teaspoon vanilla extract

Bring first 5 ingredients to a boil in a saucepan; boil, stirring constantly, 5 minutes. Remove from heat, and stir in morsels, nuts, and vanilla. Pour mixture into a greased 8-inch square pan. Cut firm fudge into squares.

Rocky Road Candy

2 cups (12 ounces) semisweet chocolate morsels	¾ cup peanut butter
2 cups (12 ounces) butterscotch morsels	10 ounces miniature marshmallows
	¾ cup Spanish peanuts

Combine morsels and peanut butter in a medium bowl. Microwave at MEDIUM (50 percent power) 3 to 4 minutes or until morsels are soft, stirring occasionally. Stir well. Add marshmallows and peanuts; spread into a greased 13- x 9-inch pan. Cool and cut into squares.

Peanut Clusters

2 cups (12 ounces) butterscotch morsels	1 cup (6 ounces) semisweet chocolate morsels
	12 ounces Spanish peanuts

Combine morsels in a 2-quart baking dish. Microwave at MEDIUM (60 percent power) until melted, stirring once during cooking. Stir in peanuts. Drop mixture by teaspoonfuls onto wax paper or aluminum foil. Let stand until firm.

Pecan Toffee

½ cup margarine	3 tablespoons water
½ cup butter	1 cup chopped pecans
1 cup sugar	

Combine first 4 ingredients in an electric skillet; cook at HIGH just until mixture is caramel colored. Add pecans, and quickly pour into a warm jellyroll pan; spread thin. Cool toffee, and break into pieces.

Date Balls

¾ cup butter or margarine	2 cups crisp rice cereal
1½ cups sugar	1 cup chopped nuts
1 small box dates	Powdered sugar

Cook first 3 ingredients in a saucepan over medium heat until sugar and butter melt. Add cereal and nuts. With greased hands, roll into 1-inch balls. Roll balls in powdered sugar. Chill and serve.

Festive Orange Balls

16 ounces vanilla wafers, crushed	¼ cup butter or margarine, melted
1 (8-ounce) can orange juice	½ cup chopped nuts
1 cup powdered sugar	Flaked coconut

Combine all ingredients, and roll into 1-inch balls. Roll balls in coconut. Chill and serve.

Oatmeal Fudge

2	cups sugar	½	cup butter or margarine
3	heaping teaspoons cocoa	½	cup peanut butter
½	cup milk	2	cups regular oats
1	tablespoon vanilla extract		

Bring first 3 ingredients to a boil in a saucepan over medium-high heat. Boil 5 minutes. Remove from heat, and stir in remaining ingredients. Set pan in cold water, and stir until thickened. Spoon onto wax paper to cool.

Mint Patties

⅓	cup light corn syrup	1	(16-ounce) package powdered sugar
⅓	cup butter or margarine, softened		Liquid food coloring (any color)
1	teaspoon peppermint		Pecan halves
½	teaspoon salt		

Combine all ingredients. Knead until smooth. Add desired food coloring, and shape into 1½-inch patties. Top with pecan halves.

Sweetened Condensed Milk

1	cup powdered milk	3	tablespoons melted margarine
⅓	cup boiling water		Pinch of salt
⅔	cup sugar		

Process all ingredients in a blender until smooth. Serve or chill.

'Sees' Candy

2 (16-ounce) packages
   powdered sugar
2 teaspoons vanilla extract
   Dash of salt
1 cup butter
1 can sweetened condensed
   milk

2 cups chopped nuts
1 cup flaked coconut
18 (1-ounce) squares semisweet
   chocolate
1 block paraffin wax

Combine first 5 ingredients. Add nuts and coconut. Chill 1 hour. Roll into 1-inch balls. Place on cookie sheets, and freeze. Melt chocolate and wax in top of a double boiler; dip each ball using wooden picks. Place on wax paper to cool.

Custard Sauce

4 eggs yolks
⅓ cup sugar
⅛ teaspoon salt

2 cups milk
1 teaspoon vanilla extract

Whisk together first 3 ingredients in a heavy 2-quart saucepan over low heat. Gradually stir in milk, and cook, stirring constantly, 25 minutes or until mixture thickens and coats a spoon. Stir in vanilla. Serve warm or cold over apple pie, fruitcake, fruit salad, or ice cream.

Light
&
Healthy

Lori Bierman

Liver transplant recipient,
2002

Lori has faced many health challenges in her life. Her body rejected her first liver transplant, but she received a second transplant in August 2002. At first, she couldn't absorb the anti-rejection medications, but eventually she began to respond to the medications. Today, she is the proud mother to Cameron, the miracle child she never thought she'd have.

Sweet Cinnamon-Raisin Spread

1	cup low-fat (1 percent) cottage cheese	1	tablespoon honey
2	tablespoons low-fat plain yogurt	1	tablespoon light brown sugar
		¼	teaspoon ground cinnamon
		½	cup raisins

Process cheese in a blender, stopping to scrape down sides, 1 minute or until very smooth. Scrape into a small bowl. Stir in yogurt, honey, sugar, and cinnamon until blended. Stir in raisins. Cover and chill at least 2 hours.

Low-Calorie Baked Apples

1	can diet soft drink	8	apples

Core apples, and place in a 13- x 9-inch baking dish; pour soft drink over apples. Bake at 350° until apples are soft, basting often with pan juices.

Meatless Lasagna

1	medium onion, chopped		Dash of salt and pepper
1	medium green bell pepper, chopped and seeded	1	teaspoon sugar
			Pressed garlic to taste
2	medium zucchini, chopped	2½	cups water
¼	cup water	18	prebaked lasagna noodles
1	(16-ounce) can tomatoes, undrained	1	pound fat-free mozzarella cheese, shredded
1	(16-ounce) can red beans, undrained	1	(16-ounce) container fat-free cottage cheese
3	tablespoons tomato paste		

Sauté first 3 ingredients in ¼ cup water in a large nonstick skillet until tender. Drain well. Add tomatoes and next 6 ingredients. Bring mixture to a boil. Reduce heat, and simmer, stirring occasionally, 15 minutes. In a 13- x 9-inch baking dish, layer one-third of tomato mixture, half of noodles, half of mozzarella, half of cottage cheese, and one-third of tomato mixture. Top with remaining noodles, remaining cottage cheese, remaining mozzarella, and remaining tomato mixture. Bake, covered, 40 to 50 minutes. Uncover and bake 15 more minutes. Let stand 10 minutes before cutting.

Sour Cream Substitute

¼ cup water or milk
8 ounces creamed cottage
   cheese

1 tablespoon lemon juice
¼ teaspoon salt

Combine all ingredients in an airtight container. Cover or seal, and shake vigorously 50 seconds or until creamy.

Apple-Glazed Carrots

1 tablespoon butter or
   margarine
1 (16-ounce) package peeled,
   trimmed baby carrots
1 cup unsweetened apple juice

1 teaspoon honey
   Salt and pepper to taste
1 tablespoon minced green
   onion tops

Melt butter in a large nonstick skillet over medium-high heat. Add carrots; sauté 8 minutes or until they start to brown. Add apple juice and honey; bring mixture to a boil. Reduce heat, and simmer, stirring occasionally, 15 minutes or until carrots are tender and liquid is reduced to glaze. Season to taste. Sprinkle with green onions.

Low-Fat Vegetable Soup

3   medium zucchini, sliced
2   medium carrots, sliced
12 mushrooms, sliced
1   medium onion, sliced
1   (10-ounce) russet potato,
    peeled and cubed
3   (14½-ounce) cans vegetable
    broth
3   cups canned crushed
    tomatoes with added purée

1 (14½-ounce) can stewed
   tomatoes
3 tablespoons chopped fresh
   parsley
2 tablespoons chopped fresh
   cilantro
1 tablespoon chopped garlic
1 teaspoon dried basil
1 teaspoon dried oregano
   Chopped fresh parsley

Combine first 5 ingredients in a large heavy Dutch oven. Add broth and next 7 ingredients. Bring mixture to a boil. Reduce heat, and simmer 30 minutes or until vegetables are tender. Pour through a wire-mesh strainer into a large saucepan, reserving vegetables. Process 3 cups vegetables and ¼ cup cooking liquid in blender until smooth. Pour purée into cooking liquid. Return remaining vegetables to cooking liquid. Season with salt and pepper. Cook until thoroughly heated; sprinkle with chopped parsley.

Low-Profile Cheese Sauce

1 (12-ounce) container low-fat
cottage cheese
1 (5-ounce) can evaporated
skimmed milk

½ cup (2 ounces) shredded
Cheddar cheese

Process cottage cheese and milk in a blender until smooth. Place in a saucepan, and cook over low heat until heated. Add Cheddar cheese; stir until melted.

You may season your sauce with hot sauce, pepper, dry mustard, Parmesan, Worcestershire sauce, or sliced green onions.

New-Fashioned Apple Cobbler

1 tablespoon cornstarch
½ cup apple juice, divided
5 cups peeled and sliced
cooking apples
⅓ cup firmly packed brown
sugar
½ teaspoon ground cinnamon

¼ teaspoon ground nutmeg
¼ teaspoon ground cloves
Vegetable cooking spray
½ cup all-purpose flour
2 tablespoons corn oil
margarine
1-2 tablespoons cold water

Combine cornstarch and ¼ cup apple juice; set aside.

Combine remaining ¼ cup apple juice and next 5 ingredients in a heavy saucepan; bring to a boil. Reduce heat, and simmer 10 minutes, stirring occasionally. Stir in cornstarch mixture; cook over medium heat, stirring constantly, until mixture begins to boil. Boil 1 minute, stirring constantly, until mixture is thickened and bubbly. Remove from heat; pour into an 8-inch square baking dish coated with cooking spray. Set aside.

Place flour in a small bowl; cut in margarine with a pastry blender until mixture resembles coarse meal. Sprinkle water evenly over surface of mixture; stir with a fork until dry ingredients are moistened. Shape into a ball; gently press between 2 sheets of heavy-duty plastic wrap into a 4-inch circle. Chill 15 minutes.

Roll dough to an 8-inch square; freeze 5 minutes. Remove top sheet of plastic wrap; cut dough into strips to fit baking dish. Arrange strips over apples in a lattice design. Bake at 425° for 30 to 35 minutes or until cobbler is bubbly and crust is golden.

Yield: 6 servings (169 calories per ½-cup serving).

Chicken Croquettes and Mushroom Sauce

6	(4-ounce) skinned, boned chicken breast halves		Vegetable cooking spray
1	stalk celery, cut into 1-inch pieces	½	cup egg substitute
		½	teaspoon salt
1	medium carrot, cut into ½-inch slices	½	teaspoon pepper
		2	tablespoons cornstarch
1	small onion, cut into ½-inch slices	½	cup skim milk
		½	cup reduced-sodium cracker crumbs
2	cups water	¼	teaspoon paprika
½	cup diced celery		Mushroom Sauce
½	cup diced onion		

Combine first 5 ingredients in a large saucepan; bring to a boil. Cover, reduce heat, and cook 15 minutes or until chicken is tender. Remove chicken from broth; strain broth, reserving 1½ cups. Set aside.

Position knife blade in food processor bowl. Place chicken in processor bowl; process 45 seconds or until chicken is finely chopped, but not smooth. Set aside.

Sauté ½ cup diced celery and ½ cup diced onion in a large skillet coated with cooking spray. Remove from heat. Stir in chicken, egg substitute, salt, and pepper.

Combine cornstarch, milk, and ½ cup reserved broth in a small saucepan. Cook over medium heat, stirring constantly, until mixture begins to boil; boil 1 minute, stirring constantly. Stir sauce into chicken mixture; shape into 6 croquettes. Combine cracker crumbs and paprika; roll croquettes in crumbs, and place on a baking sheet coated with cooking spray. Bake at 375° for 30 minutes or until croquettes are thoroughly heated. Serve with Mushroom Sauce. Yield: 6 servings (228 calories per croquette with ¼ cup Mushroom Sauce).

Mushroom Sauce

2	cups sliced fresh mushrooms	1	cup reserved chicken broth
2	tablespoons reduced-calorie margarine, melted	⅛	teaspoon salt
		¼	teaspoon pepper
2	tablespoons all-purpose flour		

Sauté mushrooms in margarine in a saucepan over medium heat. Add flour, stirring until smooth. Cook 1 minute, stirring constantly. Gradually stir in chicken broth; cook over medium heat, stirring constantly, until thickened and bubbly. Stir in salt and pepper. Yield: 1½ cups (9 calories per tablespoon).

Sweet-and-Sour Chicken

2   tablespoons cornstarch
2   tablespoons granulated
     brown sugar substitute
     sweetened with saccharin
1   tablespoon low-sodium
     Worcestershire sauce
¾   teaspoon ground ginger
¼   teaspoon garlic powder
1½   cups unsweetened pineapple
     juice

¼   cup low-sodium soy sauce
¼   cup wine vinegar
¼   cup reduced-calorie ketchup
     Vegetable cooking spray
3   cups cubed uncooked chicken
½   cup julienne-cut sweet red
     pepper
½   julienne-cut green pepper
3   cups hot cooked rice (cooked
     without salt or fat)

Combine first 9 ingredients in a medium bowl; stir well.

Coat a nonstick skillet with cooking spray; place over medium-high heat until hot. Add chicken, and sauté 5 minutes. Add sweet red pepper and green pepper; sauté 2 minutes. Gradually stir cornstarch mixture into chicken mixture. Cook over medium heat, stirring until thickened and bubbly. Serve over rice. Yield: 6 servings (299 calories per ⅔ cup mixture and ½ cup rice).

Creamy Broccoli Soup

1   (10-ounce) package frozen
     chopped broccoli, thawed
2¼   cups skim milk
1   tablespoon reduced-calorie
     margarine
1   (2-ounce) envelope instant
     mashed potato flakes

2   teaspoons instant minced
     onion
1   (10½-ounce) can ready-to-
     serve, no-salt-added chicken
     broth
¼   teaspoon salt
¼   teaspoon pepper

Cook broccoli according to package directions, omitting salt; set aside.

Combine milk and margarine in a medium saucepan; cook over medium heat, stirring constantly, until thoroughly heated (do not boil). Stir in potato flakes and onion. Place in container of an electric blender; add broccoli, and process 30 seconds. Scrape down sides; process an additional 30 seconds or until almost smooth. Return to saucepan.

Stir in broth, salt, and pepper; simmer 10 minutes, stirring often. Yield: 4 servings (142 calories per 1-cup serving).

Fruit Cup

2   (16-ounce) cans sliced
    peaches, packed in extra light
    syrup
1   (8-ounce) can unsweetened
    pineapple tidbits, undrained
2   cups sliced strawberries
1½ cups sliced bananas

1   teaspoon orange-flavored
    breakfast beverage crystals
    sweetened with aspartame
1   (0.9-ounce) package vanilla-
    flavored instant pudding mix
    sweetened with aspartame

Drain peaches; cut into bite-size pieces. Combine peaches and remaining ingredients; stir gently until all fruit is coated. Cover and chill thoroughly. Yield: 11 servings (84 calories per ½-cup serving).

Copyright 1991 Southern Living, Inc.
Reprinted with permission

Chicken In Foil

2   (6-ounce) skinned chicken
    breast halves
¼   cup sliced onion
½   tomato, sliced
1   medium-size baking potato,
    sliced
1   small carrot, sliced

1   stalk celery, sliced
    Freshly ground pepper to
    taste
⅛   teaspoon dried whole
    tarragon
1   teaspoon lemon juice

Cut two 15- x 12-inch pieces of heavy-duty aluminum foil; place a chicken breast in center of each. Top with onion and remaining ingredients. Wrap well; place on baking sheet. Bake at 350° for 1 hour. Yield: 2 servings (221 calories per serving).

Copyright 1991 Southern Living, Inc.
Reprinted with permission

Chili Popcorn

1   tablespoon margarine, melted
½   teaspoon chili powder
⅛   teaspoon salt
⅛   teaspoon garlic powder

⅛   teaspoon paprika
6   cups popped corn (popped
    without salt or fat)

Combine first 5 ingredients, and drizzle over warm popcorn. Yield: 6 servings (41 calories per 1-cup serving).

Copyright 1991 Southern Living, Inc.
Reprinted with permission

Freezer Bran Muffins

3 cups shreds of wheat bran cereal	2 cups buttermilk
½ cup raisins	¼ cup molasses
½ cup vegetable oil	2¼ cups whole wheat flour
1 cup boiling water	2½ teaspoons baking soda
½ cup egg substitute	1½ tablespoons sugar
	Vegetable cooking spray

Combine first 4 ingredients in a large bowl; stir well, and let stand 10 minutes until cereal is moistened. Combine egg substitute, buttermilk, and molasses; add to cereal mixture, stirring well.

Combine flour, soda, and sugar; add to cereal mixture, stirring just until dry ingredients are moistened. Cover batter, and let stand at room temperature 15 minutes. Spoon batter into muffin pans coated with vegetable cooking spray, filling two-thirds full. Bake at 400° for 18 to 20 minutes or until done. Yield: 2 dozen (142 calories each).

Blueberry Muffins

⅓ cup reduced-calorie margarine, softened	¼ teaspoon baking soda
¼ cup granulated sugar substitute sweetened with saccharin	¼ teaspoon salt
	1 egg
	½ cup skim milk
1¼ cups all-purpose flour	1 cup frozen blueberries, thawed and drained
1 teaspoon baking powder	Vegetable cooking spray

Beat margarine at medium speed of an electric mixer; gradually add sugar substitute, beating well.

Combine flour, baking powder, soda, and salt. Combine egg and milk; stir well. Add flour and milk mixtures alternately to creamed mixture, beginning and ending with flour mixture. Mix just until blended. Gently stir in blueberries.

Spoon batter into miniature (1¾-inch) muffin pans coated with cooking spray, filling two-thirds full. Bake at 375° for 15 to 20 minutes or until muffins are done. Yield: 2 dozen miniature muffins (50 calories per muffin).

Applesauce Muffins

1	cup all-purpose flour	¾	cup nonfat buttermilk
1	cup regular oats, uncooked	¾	cup unsweetened applesauce
¼	cup unprocessed oat bran	¼	cup vegetable oil
¼	cup sugar	1	teaspoon vanilla extract
1½	teaspoons baking soda		Vegetable cooking spray
1	teaspoon baking powder	1	tablespoon sugar
⅔	cup raisins or chopped dates	½	teaspoon ground cinnamon
2	egg whites, lightly beaten		

Combine first 7 ingredients in a large bowl; make a well in center of mixture. Combine egg whites and next 4 ingredients; add to dry ingredients, stirring just until moistened.

Spoon ¼ cup batter into muffin pan coated with cooking spray. Combine 1 tablespoon sugar and cinnamon; sprinkle on top of muffin batter. Bake at 400° for 20 minutes. Yield: 16 muffins (147 calories each).

Cornmeal Muffins

1	cup yellow cornmeal	1	teaspoon sugar
1	cup all-purpose flour	¼	cup egg substitute or 2 egg
2	teaspoons baking powder		whites
1	teaspoon baking soda	¼	cup vegetable oil
½	teaspoon salt		Vegetable cooking spray

Combine cornmeal, flour, baking powder, soda, salt, and sugar in a large bowl; make a well in center of mixture. Combine egg substitute, yogurt, and oil; add to dry ingredients, stirring just until moistened.

Spoon mixture into muffin pans coated with cooking spray, filling three-fourths full. Bake at 425° for 12 to 14 minutes or until golden brown. Remove muffins from pans immediately. Yield: 1½ dozen (96 calories per muffin).

Corn Tortilla Chips

10 (6-inch) tortillas   Cold water

Cut 3 circles from each tortilla, using a 2½-inch biscuit cutter. Dip rounds in water; drain on paper towels. Place rounds in a single layer on an ungreased baking sheet. Bake at 350° for 10 minutes or until chips are crisp and begin to brown. Remove from oven, and let cool. Yield: 26 chips (12 calories per chip).

Bagel Chips

6   plain bagels   Butter-flavored vegetable
                                          cooking spray

Using an electric slicer or serrated knife, horizontally cut each bagel into 6 (¼-inch) slices. Arrange slices in a single layer on wire racks; place racks on baking sheets. Coat slices with cooking spray. Bake at 325° for 12 to 15 minutes or until crisp and lightly browned. Remove from oven; let cool. Store in an airtight container. Yield: 3 dozen (28 calories per chip).

Parmesan Cheese Bagel Chips:
Sprinkle 2 teaspoons of grated Parmesan cheese evenly over bagel chips coated with cooking spray (28 calories per chip).

Lemon-and-Herb Bagel Chips:
Sprinkle 2 teaspoons salt-free lemon-and-herb spice blend evenly over bagel chips coated with cooking spray (29 calories per chip).

Garlic Bagel Chips:
Sprinkle 1 teaspoon garlic powder evenly over bagel chips coated with cooking spray (28 calories per chip).

Cinnamon-and-Sugar Bagel Chips:
Combine ¼ teaspoon ground cinnamon and 1½ teaspoons sugar; sprinkle mixture evenly over bagel chips coated with cooking spray (29 calories per chip).

Vegetable Nachos

1 cup diced tomato	2 teaspoons white vinegar
¼ cup diced green pepper	¼ teaspoon garlic powder
2 tablespoons sliced green onions	⅛ teaspoon freshly ground pepper
2 tablespoons chopped ripe olives	Corn Tortilla Chips
2 tablespoons chopped green chiles	¼ cup (1 ounce) shredded 40-percent-less-fat sharp Cheddar cheese

Combine first 8 ingredients. Spoon 2 teaspoons vegetable mixture on each tortilla chip; divide cheese evenly among chips. Broil 6 inches from heat 1 minute or until cheese melts. Yield: 26 appetizers (18 calories each).

Copyright 1991 Southern Living, Inc.
Reprinted with permission

Sloppy Toms

Vegetable cooking spray	½ teaspoon dried whole basil
1 pound raw ground turkey	½ teaspoon dried whole oregano
¾ cup chopped onion	¼ teaspoon salt
⅔ cup chopped green pepper	¼ teaspoon pepper
2 cloves garlic, minced	1¼ cups shredded zucchini
1 (8-ounce) can no-salt-added tomato sauce	⅔ cup shredded carrot
¼ cup reduced-calorie catsup	6 whole wheat hamburger buns
1 teaspoon chili powder	

Coat a large, nonstick skillet with cooking spray; place skillet over medium-high heat. Add ground turkey, onion, green pepper, and garlic; cook until browned, stirring well to crumble turkey. Drain well on paper towels. Return turkey mixture to skillet; add tomato sauce and remaining ingredients except buns. Cook over medium heat 10 minutes, stirring occasionally. Divide mixture evenly among hamburger buns; cover with top half of bun. Yield: 6 servings (318 calories per serving).

Copyright 1991 Southern Living, Inc.
Reprinted with permission

Breaded Herbed Fish Fillets

½ cup fine, dry breadcrumbs
¼ cup all-purpose flour
2 teaspoons chicken-flavored bouillon granules
1 teaspoon dried onion flakes
1 teaspoon paprika
1 teaspoon dried parsley flakes
½ teaspoon dried whole dillweed
½ teaspoon dried whole thyme
¼ teaspoon garlic powder
4 (4-ounce) farm-raised catfish fillets
   Butter-flavored vegetable cooking spray

Combine first 9 ingredients in a shallow dish. Coat fillets with cooking spray; dredge in breadcrumb mixture. Place fillets on a broiler pan coated with cooking spray; bake, uncovered, at 400° for 20 minutes or until fish flakes easily when tested with a fork. Serve immediately. Yield: 4 servings (225 calories per fillet).

Supreme Bean Salad

1 (16-ounce) can no-salt-added green beans, drained
1 (16-ounce) can yellow wax beans, drained
1 (10-ounce) package frozen English peas, thawed
1 cup chopped green pepper
1 cup thinly sliced purple onion
1 (2-ounce) jar diced pimiento, drained
1 teaspoon minced fresh garlic
¾ cup white vinegar
1 tablespoon vegetable oil
½ teaspoon salt
½ teaspoon pepper
16 packets sugar substitute sweetened with aspartame or 8 packets sweetened with acesulfame-K or saccharin

Combine first 7 ingredients in a large bowl; set aside. Combine vinegar, oil, salt, and pepper in a small saucepan; bring to a boil. Remove from heat; stir in sugar substitute. Pour over vegetables; toss gently. Cover and chill 3 hours, stirring occasionally. Drain before serving. Yield: 7 servings (106 calories per 1-cup serving).

Four-Flavor Pound Cake

Vegetable cooking spray
1¾ cups sifted cake flour
2 teaspoons baking powder
¼ teaspoon salt
¾ cup sugar
½ vegetable oil
½ cup skim milk
½ teaspoon grated lemon rind
¼ teaspoon almond extract
¼ teaspoon rum extract
¼ teaspoon lemon extract
1 teaspoon vanilla extract
4 egg whites, stiffly beaten
Fresh strawberries

Coat the bottom of an 8½- x 4½- x 3-inch loaf pan with cooking spray; dust with flour, and set aside.

Combine 1¾ cups flour and next 3 ingredients in a large bowl. Add oil and milk; beat at medium speed of an electric mixer until batter is smooth (batter will be thick). Add lemon rind and next 4 ingredients; fold in about one-third of egg whites. Gently fold in remaining egg whites.

Pour batter into pan. Bake at 350° for 40 minutes or until a wooden pick inserted in center comes out clean.

Cool in pan 10 minutes; remove from pan, and cool on a wire rack. Serve ¾ cup fresh strawberries with each slice. Yield: 16 servings (183 calories per ½-inch slice and ¾ cup strawberries).

Green Beans and Potatoes

4 medium-size red potatoes, cut into eighths
2 (16-ounce) cans no-salt-added green beans, drained
1 medium onion, sliced and separated into rings
2 teaspoons beef-flavored bouillon granules
½ teaspoon garlic powder
¼ teaspoon pepper
1 cup water

Layer all ingredients in a large saucepan in the order given; bring to a boil. Cover, reduce heat, and simmer 20 minutes or until potatoes are fork tender. Yield: 6 servings (143 calories per 1-cup serving).

Angel Food Trifle

1 (16-ounce) package angel food cake mix
⅓ cup sugar
¼ cup cornstarch
¼ teaspoon salt
2 cups skim milk
¼ cup egg substitute

1 teaspoon grated lemon rind
¼ cup lemon juice
2 (8-ounce) cartons vanilla low-fat yogurt
2 cups sliced strawberries
3 kiwifruit, sliced
3 strawberry fans

Prepare cake mix according to package directions. Cut into bite-size cubes; set aside. Combine sugar, cornstarch, and salt in a saucepan; gradually add milk, stirring well. Cook over medium heat until mixture begins to thicken, stirring constantly. Remove from heat; gradually add egg substitute, stirring constantly with a wire whisk. Cook over medium-low heat 2 minutes, stirring constantly. Remove from heat; cool slightly. Stir in lemon rind and lemon juice; chill. Fold yogurt into cream mixture; set aside. Place one-third of cake in bottom of a 16-cup trifle bowl. Spoon one-third of custard over cake; arrange half each of strawberry slices and kiwi slices around lower edge of bowl and over custard. Repeat procedure with remaining ingredients, ending with strawberry fans on top. Cover and chill 3 to 4 hours. Yield: 15 servings (198 calories per ⅔-cup serving).

Twice Baked Cottage-Style Potatoes

2 medium-size baking potatoes
½ cup low-fat cottage cheese
2 tablespoons skim milk
2 teaspoons sliced green onions

⅛ teaspoon salt
⅛ teaspoon pepper
⅛ teaspoon paprika
Garnish: fresh parsley sprigs

Wash potatoes; prick several times with a fork. Bake at 400° for 1 hour or until done. Let cool to touch. Slice skin away from top of each potato. Carefully scoop out pulp, leaving shells intact. Set aside. Mash pulp.

Combine cottage cheese and milk in container of an electric blender or food processor; process until smooth. Add cottage cheese mixture, green onions, salt, and pepper to potato pulp; stir well. Stuff shells with potato mixture; sprinkle with paprika. Bake at 400° for 10 minutes or until thoroughly heated. Garnish, if desired. Yield: 2 servings (155 calories each).

Black Beans and Rice

1¼ cups dried black beans
Vegetable cooking spray
1 cup chopped onion
1 cup chopped green pepper
5 cloves garlic, minced
½ teaspoon salt
½ teaspoon pepper
¼ teaspoon crushed red pepper

1 tablespoon red wine vinegar
3 cups water
1 (6-ounce) can tomato paste
3 cups hot cooked rice (cooked without salt or fat)
½ cup chopped tomato
¼ cup sliced green onions
4 teaspoons plain nonfat yogurt

Sort and wash beans; place in a Dutch oven. Cover with water 2 inches above beans; let soak 8 hours. Drain.

Coat a Dutch oven with cooking spray; place over medium-high heat until hot. Add chopped onion, green pepper, and garlic; sauté until tender. Add beans, salt, and next 4 ingredients, and bring mixture to a boil. Cover, reduce heat, and simmer 1½ hours or until beans are tender, stirring occasionally. Add tomato paste; cook an additional 15 minutes.

Serve over rice. Top each serving with tomato, green onions, and yogurt. Yield: 4 servings (468 calories per 1 cup beans, ¾ cup rice, 2 tablespoons tomato, 1 tablespoon green onions, and 1 teaspoon yogurt).

Company Broccoli-and-Zucchini Sauté

3 large bunches broccoli
5 small zucchini (about 8 ounces each)
1 bunch green onions
Vegetable oil

Salt
⅔ cup water
1 teaspoon dried basil
1 tablespoon soy sauce
Lettuce leaves

Cut broccoli into 2-inch pieces. Cut zucchini into ½-inch slices. Cut each green onion into 2-inch pieces. Sauté green onions in ⅓ cup hot oil in an 8-quart Dutch oven medium heat 3 minutes or until tender. With rubber spatula, stir in broccoli and 1¼ teaspoons salt until broccoli is coated with oil. Add water; cover and cook, stirring occasionally, 5 to 8 minutes or until broccoli is crisp-tender. Remove from vegetables and liquid to a bowl. Sauté zucchini, basil, and 1 teaspoon salt in ¼ cup hot oil over medium heat until zucchini is crisp-tender. Return broccoli mixture to Dutch oven; add soy sauce. Stir well. Line a serving platter with lettuce leaves. Spoon vegetables onto platter. Serve hot or cold. Serves 16 (100 calories per serving).

Low-Fat Round Steak

1   round steak, trimmed and cut   Salt and pepper to taste
    into 3 or 4 pieces   3   beef bouillon cubes
    Water

Brown steak in a skillet over medium heat (without oil) almost to burning. Add water to cover; reduce heat to low. Add salt and pepper and bouillon cubes. Simmer 1½ hours. Keep water level over steak throughout cooking time. Use broth for gravy.

Lemon Chicken Breasts

4   skinned chicken breasts   1   large green bell pepper, cut
1-2 large lemons   into 8 pieces
    Garlic powder to taste   2   medium potatoes, quartered
1   large tomato, cut into quarters   lengthwise

Sprinkle chicken with lemon juice and garlic powder. Sprinkle vegetables with lemon and garlic. Arrange chicken and vegetables in a roasting pan. Cover tightly with aluminum foil. Bake at 450° for 30 to 35 minutes.

Low-Cholesterol Quiche

1   pound turkey sausage,   1   (9-inch) unbaked pie shell
    browned   2   (8-ounce) cartons vegetable
1   onion, chopped   egg substitute
2   cups (8 ounces) mozzarella   ½   cup skim milk

Layer sausage, onion, and cheese into pie shell. Pour egg substitute and milk over sausage mixture. Bake at 375° for 45 minutes or until set.

Sugar-Free Ambrosia

6   naval oranges   3   bananas, sliced
1   (16-ounce) can crushed   Grated coconut
    pineapple (in juice)

Peel oranges, and remove membrane. Combine orange sections, pineapple, and banana in a serving bowl. Sprinkle with coconut.

Brown Rice Pilaf

2   cups ready-to-serve, no-salt-
    added chicken broth
1   cup brown rice, uncooked
½   cup grated carrot
½   cup finely chopped celery
¼   cup finely sliced green onions

1   clove garlic, minced
½   teaspoon salt
¼   teaspoon red pepper
3   tablespoons slivered almonds,
    toasted

Bring broth to a boil in a heavy saucepan; stir in rice and remaining ingredient except almonds. Cover, reduce heat, and simmer 25 to 30 minutes or until liquid is absorbed. Stir in almonds. Yield: 8 servings (111 calories per ½-cup serving).

Green Pepper-Onion-Carrot Medley

8   medium green bell peppers
4   medium onions
1   (16-ounce) bag carrots
1½ teaspoons salt

1   teaspoon dried basil
½   teaspoon coarsely ground
    black pepper
3   tablespoons vegetable oil

Cut green peppers into strips. Thinly slice onions, and cut carrots into matchsticks. Cook all ingredients in hot oil in an 8-quart Dutch oven over medium-high heat, stirring often, until vegetables are tender. Serves 8 (125 calories per serving).

Low-Fat Cabbage Soup

1   (12-ounce) can diced
    tomatoes, undrained
2   cups water
3   cups shredded cabbage
½   cup diced celery
1   teaspoon dried parsley flakes
1   dried onion soup mix

1   teaspoon sugar
    Dash of garlic salt
    Salt and pepper to taste
1   cup French-style green beans
1   cup (4 ounces) sliced
    mushrooms with liquid

Combine first 11 ingredients in a large stockpot. Cook over medium heat until vegetables are tender. Add mushrooms and green beans. Cook until thoroughly heated.

Summer Fruit Bowl

2	cups water	1	small cantaloupe
1½	cups sugar	6	large plums
3	tablespoons lime juice	4	large nectarines
¾	cup mint leaves, minced	1	pound seedless green grapes
1	(20-pound) watermelon		

Cook first 3 ingredients in a 2-quart saucepan over medium heat 15 minutes or until mixture becomes a light syrup. Stir in mint; cover and chill. Cut watermelon and cantaloupe into bite-size pieces; discard seeds. Cut plums and nectarines into wedges. Combine cut fruit and grapes, and arrange in a very large bowl. Pour chilled syrup mixture through wire-mesh strainer over fruit. Toss gently. Cover and chill, stirring occasionally. Serves 20 (175 calories per serving.

Grilled Chicken Sesame

1	tablespoon sesame seeds, toasted	1	tablespoon sherry
2	teaspoons grated ginger	4	(4-ounce) skinned, boned chicken breast halves
2	tablespoons honey		Vegetable cooking spray
1	tablespoon reduced-sodium soy sauce		

Combine first 5 ingredients in a small bowl. Set aside. Flatten chicken pieces to ¼-inch thickness using a mallet or rolling pin. Spray grill with cooking spray. Grill chicken over medium-hot coals 4 minutes each side, basting frequently with soy sauce mixture. Transfer to serving platter. Serves 4; chicken breast half per serving.

Reprinted with permission from the Kidney Dialysis Association.

Bow-Tie Pasta Salad

2	cups cooked bow-tie pasta	2	tablespoons minced onion
¼	cups chopped celery	⅛	teaspoon pepper
2	tablespoons chopped green bell pepper	⅔	cup mayonnaise
2	tablespoons shredded carrot	½	teaspoon sugar
		1	tablespoon lemon juice

Mix pasta, celery, green pepper, carrot, onion, and pepper in a bowl. Stir in remaining ingredients. Chill. Serves 8 (⅓ cup per serving).

Reprinted with permission from the Kidney Dialysis Association.

Orange Chiffon Cheesecake

2 cups graham cracker crumbs
½ cup reduced-fat margarine, melted
1 cup orange juice
1 envelope unflavored gelatin
12 ounces reduced-fat cream cheese, softened
1 cup part-skim ricotta cheese
12 packets artificial sweetener
1 package reduced-calorie whipped topping mix
½ cup skim milk
2 medium oranges, peeled, seeded, and chopped

Coat a pie plate with vegetable cooking spray. Combine crumbs and melted margarine; press into bottom and up sides of pie plate. Bake at 350° for 8 to 10 minutes. Pour orange juice into a saucepan; sprinkle gelatin over juice. Let stand 1 minute; heat, stirring constantly, until gelatin dissolves (about 3 minutes). Blend cream cheese and ricotta in a large bowl until smooth. Stir in sweetener. Add gelatin mixture, and blend until smooth. Prepare whipped topping according to package directions, substituting milk for water. Fold into cream cheese mixture. Stir in chopped orange. Spoon into prepared crust. Garnish with orange wedges, if desired. Chill 6 hours.

Apple Cake
With Warm Honey Sauce

3 tablespoons unsalted margarine
½ cup sugar
½ cup honey
1 egg
2 cups flour
1 teaspoon baking powder
½ teaspoon baking soda
¼ teaspoon nutmeg
⅓ cup lemon juice
3 cups diced, peeled apples
2½ teaspoons cornstarch
½ cup honey
⅓ cup water
1 tablespoon grated lemon peel
3 tablespoons lemon juice
1 tablespoon unsalted margarine
Dash of nutmeg

Preheat oven to 350°F. Cream margarine and sugar. Add honey and beat well. Add egg and mix. Beat in flour, baking powder, baking soda, and nutmeg. Stir in lemon juice and apples. Pour into a greased 9-inch square baking pan. Bake for 55 to 60 minutes. For sauce, mix cornstarch, honey, and water together in a small saucepan. Add lemon rind. Cook over moderate heat for about 5 minutes or until thick, stirring occasionally. Remove from heat and stir in lemon juice, margarine, and nutmeg. Serves 9; 1 3-inch square of cake with 2½ tablespoons sauce per serving.

Reprinted with permission from the Kidney Dialysis Association.

How Much Fiber Is In Your Food?

	Serving Size	Fiber (g)
Breads and Cereals		
Barley, uncooked	⅓ cup	5.0
Bulgur wheat, cooked	½ cup	1.5
Grits, corn, quick	½ cup	0.3
Hominy, canned	½ cup	2.0
Oatmeal, cooked	½ cup	1.1
Oat bran, uncooked	⅓ cup	4.1
Rice, brown, cooked	½ cup	1.7
Rice, white, cooked	½ cup	0.5
Whole wheat bread	1 slice	2.1
Fruits		
Apple, raw	1 medium	4.3
Applesauce, canned, Unsweetened	½ cup	1.8
Apricots, dried	½ cup	5.1
Banana, raw	1 medium	1.9
Blackberries, raw	½ cup	5.3
Blueberries, raw	½ cup	2.2
Dates, dried	½ cup	7.8
Kiwifruit, raw	1 each	2.4
Nectarine, raw	1 medium	2.2
Orange, raw	1 medium	3.1
Peach, raw	1 medium	1.4
Pear, raw	1 medium	4.3
Prunes, dried	½ cup	5.8
Raisins, dried	½ cup	3.8
Strawberries, raw	½ cup	1.9
Vegetables		
Artichoke	1 each	1.1
Beans, green, cooked	½ cup	1.2
Broccoli, cooked	½ cup	2.0
Brussels sprouts, cooked	½ cup	3.4
Cabbage, cooked	½ cup	0.8
Carrots, cooked	½ cup	1.5
Okra, cooked	½ cup	0.6
Potato, with skin, baked	1 medium	3.6
Spinach, cooked	½ cup	2.4
Squash, cooked	½ cup	1.4
Sweet potato, cooked	1 medium	3.4
Tomato, raw	1 medium	1.6

	Serving Size	Fiber (g)
Legumes		
Black beans, cooked	½ cup	3.6
Black-eyed peas, cooked	½ cup	1.5
Kidney beans, cooked	½ cup	3.2
Lentils, cooked	½ cup	4.0
Navy beans, cooked	½ cup	3.3
Split peas, cooked	½ cup	2.3
Nuts and Seeds		
Almonds, blanched	¼ cup	2.9
Cashews, dry roasted	¼ cup	2.1
Peanuts, dry roasted	¼ cup	2.9
Peanut butter, chunky	¼ cup	4.3
Pecans, raw	¼ cup	1.8

Nibble Your Way to Better Nutrition

Remember when eating between meals was considered a bad habit? Nowadays nutritionists are recommending eating six or eight small meals each day instead of three large ones to help control weight and possibly lower cholesterol levels. Frequent eating tames hunger pangs so that you're not ravenous at meals. And it gives the body a chance to metabolize food better.

Just by adding chili powder and garlic powder to plain popcorn it becomes anything but plain in Chili Popcorn. Other healthy options for snack food that you and your kids can prepare can be found on pages 141, 143 and 144. Serve them with a glass of juice or milk.

Trim Calories Without Sacrificing Sweetness

Each American eats nearly 130 pounds of sugar each year. With this craving for sweets added to our desire for low-calorie meals, a growing interest in sugar substitutes is at an all-time high.

Saccharin, the one most widely used, has been around for more than 90 years. It's very stable and can be heated without breaking down, making it ideal for cooking and baking. At 300 times the sweetening power of sugar, it takes only a pinch to sweeten a recipe. Familiar brands are Sweet 'N Low and Sugar Twin.

The safety of saccharin has been the subject of extensive scientific research. The National Cancer Institute conducted one of the largest studies on saccharin and concluded that there was "no evidence of increased risk with long-term use of saccharin in any form, or with the use that began decades ago."

One of the most popular sweeteners on the market today is aspartame, brand named Equal. It is made from two amino acids found naturally in foods and has about 180 times the sweetness of sugar. Its sugar like taste sweetens and enhances flavors with very little aftertaste, but it loses its sweetness when heated, making it unsuitable for cooking or baking.

The newest sweetener on the market is acesulfame-K know by the commercial name Sweet One. Chemically, acesulfame-K is similar to saccharin, and like saccharin, it can be used in cooking and baking. It is about 200 times sweeter that sugar and has less of an aftertaste than saccharin.

Recipes for baked items made with sugar substitutes generally do not have the same texture and volume as those prepared with sugar. For that reason, it's best to stick with recipes that have been tested.

Dairy Products:
Read Between The Labels

If you're concerned about the amount of fat in your diet, chances are you've switched from whole milk to 2 percent milk. After all, it's only 2 percent fat so that makes it a low-fat food, right? Wrong

Two percent milk actually contains 35 percent fat — that's enough to keep it from meeting the American Heart Association's standards for a low-fat food, which is 30 percent or less calories from fat.

The labeling terms used by the manufacturer had you thinking that 2 percent milk was low in fat. Actually 2 percent milk is 2 percent fat by weight. If you take a closer look at the nutrition label of 2 percent milk, you'll find that an 8-ounce glass has about 121 calories and 4.7 grams of fat.

To figure the percentage of fat, multiply the grams of fat (4.7) by 9 (which is the number of calories per gram of fat) to get fat calories per serving. The amount of fat calories is 42.3. Then divide this number by the total calories (121). You'll find the fat in 2 percent milk contributes 35 percent of the calories in one serving (42.3 divided by 121 equals 35 percent).

Percent of Calories from Fat
2 percent Low-Fat Milk

Nutrition Information Per Serving

Serving size	1 cup
Calories	121
Protein	8.1 grams
Carbohydrates	11.7 grams
Fat	4.7 grams

Milk and milk products are important in health-conscious eating because they are a major source of calcium. Low-fat and nonfat dairy products are as rich in calcium, protein, riboflavin, and vitamins A, B(6), and B(12) as their higher fat counterparts, and in some cases they are actually higher in calcium and protein because of the nonfat dry milk solids add to give color and body. Cottage cheese, yogurt, ricotta cheese, and even Cheddar cheese now have low-fat or nonfat versions available.

Armed with the knowledge that the key to measuring the true fat content of food is the percentage of calories from fat and not the percent of fat by weight, you'll be able to choose products that are lowest in fat. And if you're still drinking 2 percent milk, now's the time to ease down to 1 percent, ½ percent, or skim milk. The taste isn't much different, but that differences in fat content are considerable.

Do Your Heart a Favor . . .
. . . and make a move toward drinking skim milk or milk with only ½ percent or 1 percent fat. Compare the amount of fat in the different milks listed below.

	Calories Per cup	Fat grams	Percent Fat	Calcium milligrams
Skim milk	86	0.4	4%	302
½ percent	91	1.3	13%	300
1 percent	102	2.6	23%	300
2 percent	121	4.7	35%	297
Whole milk	150	8.2	49%	291
Buttermilk*	99	2.2	20%	285

*Commercial buttermilk is made from skim or 1 percent milk.

Fiber Joins The Cancer Fight

Go ahead. Take that extra helping of vegetables, fresh fruit, or whole-grain bread or cereal; these fiber-rich foods may actually decrease your chances of getting cancer.

Exactly how fiber protects us from cancer is not know, but many cancer researchers believe eating fiber-rich foods may reduce the risk of developing colon and rectal cancers. Some of the scientists suspect that because it is bulky, fiber pushes cancer-causing agents through the digestive tract and out of the body. Still another possibility under consideration these days is that fiber binds or dilutes cancer-producing agents.

The National Cancer Institute recommends boosting your dietary fiber intake to 25 to 35 grams a day — or about twice as much as most of us eat. As with many things, more isn't always better. Very large amounts of fiber, 45 grams or more, can interfere with the absorption of important minerals, such as iron and calcium.

There is an added benefit to increasing the amount of fiber in the diet — it can help you lose weight. Fiber takes up room in the stomach and makes you feel full faster. Many high-fiber foods also take longer to chew and force you to eat more slowly, and therefore eat less.

All about Rice

- Reheat cooked rice in a metal strainer or colander over a pan of steaming water. Cover the strainer with aluminum foil, and steam the rice for 15 minutes.

- Cooked rice freezes well by itself or combined with other foods that are suitable for freezing. It may be frozen for up to four months. Store cooked rice in the refrigerator for up to 1 week.

- For a tasty variation, cook rice in a flavorful liquid, such as chicken broth, beef broth, or fruit juice, instead of water.

- Herbs and spices, such as thyme, parsley, basil, and curry, add extra flavor to rice.

- Be sure to keep rice and other staples, as well as all dry foods, in their original containers or airtight ones. White rice can be stored in a container almost indefinitely.

Copyright 1991 Southern Living, Inc.
Reprinted with permission

Margarine Still Comes Out On Top

Margarine has taken a hit. For years nutritionists have told folks they could cut down on saturated fat and cholesterol by switching from butter to margarine. Now a Dutch study suggests that the trans fatty acids in margarine raise LDL-cholesterol (the "bad" cholesterol that clogs arteries) and lower HDL-cholesterol (the "good" cholesterol that helps unclog arteries). The big question to consider is whether this study makes margarine as bad a choice as butter when it comes to raising blood cholesterol levels.

Here's what happens. To make margarine from vegetable oil, the oil must undergo a process called hydrogenation. During hydrogenation some of the unsaturated fats in oil are converted from their naturally occurring cis form to a trans form. It's these trans fatty acids that are accused of raising blood cholesterol levels.

Margarines vary in the amount of trans fatty acids they contain. Stick margarines in the U.S. usually have 25 percent to 35 percent trans fatty acids; tub margarines have about 13 percent to 20 percent; and squeeze bottle margarines and spreads probably contain even less.

Copyright 1991 Southern Living, Inc.
Reprinted with permission

Index

INDEX

INDEX

N

O

P